Leonberger

Angela White

Contents

Acknowledgements

Leonbergers have attracted many people who then have become actively involved in the breed and gained a great deal of experience and knowledge over many years. I am extremely grateful to all who so readily gave support and encouragement to help me write this book. Without them it would have been an impossible feat.

Special thanks are extended to:
Fiona Karolous, whose interpretation and translation of the work of Jockers was invaluable, as was her information on the more recent early history of the breed.
Celia Peters, for her patient explanations of early history in the United Kingdom, conformation, bloodlines and the unrestricted use of her personal collection of numerous photographs and illustrations.
Angela Bursill, for imparting her vast knowledge, and also contributing to the photographs.
Glenda Smith, who patiently showed many videos explaining faults and good points in the conformation ring, as well as giving tips on handling, and delving into her photo collection for me.
Fred Inwood, for giving me my first Leonberger, Willow, and also giving Leonberger facts and figures as well as photos to help back up the history.
Lee and Lesley Gray for their help with the working Leo, giving information and especially for the help in setting up a photo session at a Leonberger fun weekend.

Thanks must go also to all who posed and lent their dogs for photos, the many Leonberger owners who responded to my pleas by sending me photographs and filling in my questionnaires regarding the health and behaviour of their Leos, and also those who responded to my internet enquiries – isn't technology a wonderful thing!

To Tom Newbould who spent several weeks searching the finished text for 'Angie's Bloomers' – thank you, Tom, for finding so many!

And last, but by no means least, Belinda and Trevor Pattrick, who gave me my first introduction to the breed when they came along to the training classes with the wonderful Disney. They have introduced me to so many Leo people and given much support.

Dedication
To Belinda and Trevor Pattrick for introducing me to this wonderful breed.

About the author

Angela White's introduction to Leonbergers was made when a couple of strangers came into the training school where she and her husband, Michael, teach all levels of obedience, from basic pet control to Championship C level Competitive Obedience, as well as various other disciplines. The class was very busy, but Angela saw the puppy Leonberger named Disney and it was 'love at first sight'.

For some time Angela had been investigating the larger breeds. When appearing in public with her demonstration Border Collies, she makes the training look so easy that people feel the Border Collie is a suitable pet. More than once she has overheard people planning to purchase one following her demonstration. Because of her great love and understanding of Collies, she knows that they are definitely not the breed for everyone, and are by no means easy for the complete beginner to train. So Angela was looking for a breed of relative intelligence that could work and accompany her on public relations outings, but whose sheer size would make people stop and think before rushing out to buy one.

Once knowing Disney, she was convinced that the Leonberger more than fitted the bill, and so the search was on for her own Leo.

Angela and Michael first saw Willow at the Leonberger Club of Great Britain show, held in the grounds of her breeder, Fred Inwood, at Kinghern Kennels, near Basingstoke in Hampshire. Michael realised that he knew Fred from his previous association with German Shepherds, and introduced himself with a view to learning more about Leonbergers.

Angela fell in love with Willow and knew that when she got her Leo she wanted one like that, not for her looks particularly, although she did find Willow stunning, but for her wonderfully alive and enthusiastic character.

Several months later, Angela received a phone call from Fred to ask if she would be interested in evaluating a young bitch whose present owner had decided to part with her. If she was suitable, perhaps Angela could take her instead of waiting for a puppy. Angela was delighted when she discovered that it was the very bitch that had caught her eye at the show.

Willow did have a few behavioural problems when she arrived at the White's household, but she was very much a teenager trying to find her way and in need of kind and positive guidance. After a few months' training she started to accompany Angela on courses, book signings, demonstrations, and to the college where Angela teaches Animal Behaviour and training; Willow was and still is an immediate hit with everyone she meets.

As an experienced author, editor of dog magazines and a self-confessed 'write-a-holic', Angela was delighted to be asked by TFH/Kingdom Books to compile a book on the breed, as this gave her a good excuse to couple her love of the breed, interest in its origins and vast knowledge of training and behaviour with her other favourite occupation – writing.

Preface

This book is designed to give an insight into one of the most majestic, gentle and appealing of breeds, the Leonberger. Anyone with an interest in the breed, whether an enthusiast, a new or even a potential Leo owner, will find the contents both enjoyable and constructive.

The book contains an interesting chapter on the origins and history of the breed but, more than that, it is a 'user's guide' as opposed to an historical work.

The contents and material are based on my experience of the most frequently-asked (and, until now, unanswered) questions from the view of the general Leo owner, the trainer, the breeder and the person who wants more from their relationship with their Leonberger.

In each area of interest, I have shown how and why the Leonberger differs from other breeds, or where it has special requirements for various reasons.

The book is ideal for those who are wanting, or are just starting out with, a new Leonberger but, as a general book of the breed, it is a must for every Leonberger owner's bookshelf.

Disney is in front, with her puppy, Crunchie, behind her.

1 Introduction

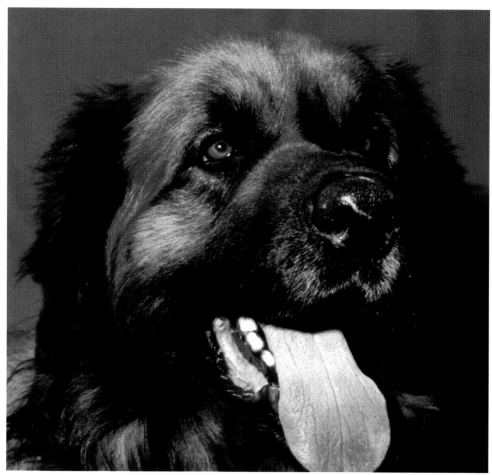

The Leonberger is bred to resemble a lion. Photograph by Pete's Photographics

Why a Leo?

The Leonberger, the Lion among dogs, is often thought of as a great, cuddly teddy bear and, indeed, there are many times when it fits that bill. But bear cubs grow into bears, and Leo pups grow into 45–69kg (100–160lb) of power and muscle.

As the author of a book on Leonbergers I can admit that I am a fan of the breed, and perhaps it is true that I find it hard to believe that anyone could *not* want a Leonberger. However, I would be the first to advise against the breed if I felt that the enquirer was not ideally suited to be a Leonberger owner. People can be very impulsive. I appear in public frequently and, prior to my Leonbergers, my companions were nearly always my beloved Border Collies. I became concerned at the attitude of some people who, just because they saw my Collies looking well behaved and beautiful at some public gathering, demonstration or training course, seemed to think that it was easy for everyone to reach that standard, irrespective of what I might say. The same happens to labradors and Golden Retrievers when they are seen as Guide Dogs for the Blind. The two years of intensive training are forgotten by people who see only the well-behaved dog in front of them. One of the original reasons I had for owning a Leonberger (apart from its ability to work and, of course, love), was that I hoped that perhaps its size might make people think twice before rushing into a purchase based purely on impulse.

Harry – a cuddly teddy bear puppy. Photograph by Pam Wells/Travelling Light

The top-winning dog of all breeds in Norway in 1992 still has a soft spot for children.
Owned and bred by Guin Gunilla and Arne Tjarnstorm.

The Leonberger was bred to resemble the lion, and it is indeed a lion of a dog. It is graceful, beautiful, charismatic, funny, gentle, loving, powerful, sometimes clumsy, sometimes obsessive, sometimes so laid back it is almost horizontal.

Leonberger puppies do resemble cuddly teddy bears, but it is a foolish breeder who does not warn prospective owners that this teddy bear will turn into a juvenile delinquent that, if not controlled and guided correctly, will soon be off the rails. Of course, some owners never experience any problem behaviour but, like any other dog owners, Leo owners come in all types: some sensible, some not so, some naive, some worldly wise, some with dog sense, some lacking in this department.

Over the last few years I have offered my services to owners who have Leonbergers with behavioural problems and surprisingly few have needed in-depth counselling. Perhaps this is because, as owners of a large dog, people are more aware of the consequences of allowing the animal to become out of control and so do their best to avoid problems by early training. This is of paramount importance with any breed of dog.

The Leonberger is a very powerful animal, and this can apply both mentally and physically. As in all things, some individuals are stronger than others, but if you meet a weak or spindly animal there is probably something wrong with it. If they catch you unprepared, most Leonbergers can pull you off your feet, and there are not many Leo owners who, hand on heart, can honestly say that at some time in their life with Leos they have not felt just a little out of control. Many do not like to admit that they have been pulled along by their Leo at some point. Having said that, once it *has* happened, normally they make doubly sure that it cannot happen again by being more aware of the circumstances that led to their Leo deciding that it would rather be elsewhere!

Generally, Leos love children and other animals, occasionally to the level of near obsession. They usually make good parents and even male Leonbergers are attentive to young puppies. In households where both parents are allowed to be with the litter, the good-natured male takes an active part in cleaning, grooming, educating and generally protecting his brood. As with any animal, however, bad experiences can easily change this. Therefore it is important to protect, guide and educate your Leo so that it can develop strong, positive traits which will serve it well and help it recover from trauma or adversity.

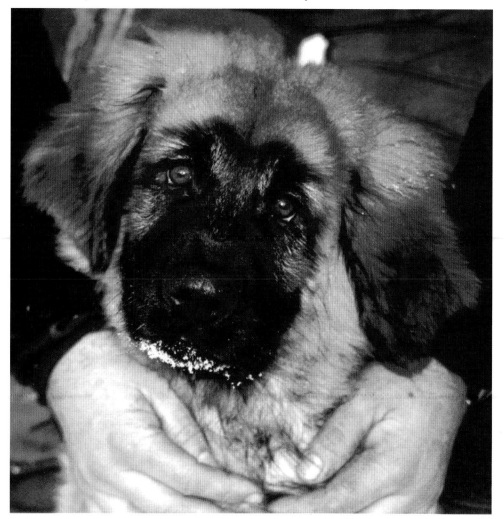

Leonbergers thrive where they are loved.

Leos usually make good parents.

Leonbergers are very loyal and need to be part of the family. They thrive where they are loved and involved in the day-to-day routine; even a mundane task such as shopping will be given an enthusiastic 'thumbs up' by your Leonberger. Their pack instinct is strong and usually they dislike living alone. This does not mean you must have more than one dog to compensate, but it is vital that your dog is involved in your life; your Leo will treat you and the family as its pack, and look to all of you to lead the way to an enjoyable and fulfilling lifestyle.

All Leonbergers need to have a good degree of kind, motivational, varied training and mental stimulus to keep them on the straight and narrow and prevent their active brains from swinging onto the wrong track. Anyone wanting a dog that requires little or no training should take up flower arranging!

Leonbergers love water and can work as enthusiastically as they can play. They excel at water rescue, carting, tracking, and any tasks that require strength and a degree of agility. They can be built up to have great stamina and, once mature and fit, can keep up with any human hiker or back-packer. Alternatively, they are very happy in the living room surrounded by the family.

The Leonberger is an excellent watch dog, with a deep bark that is most fitting to its stature. Uninvited guests are usually put off by the sheer size of the Leonberger and nature of the bark. The Leo welcomes invited guests enthusiastically (once it gets the go-ahead from you) and often helps them in by gently holding an arm in its mouth. The Leo does not usually bark for no reason.

Living with a Leo is an experience. Of course, you cannot get away from the fact that it is larger than the average pet dog but, having said that, it does not follow that it needs to live in a big house. As with any dog, its needs must be catered for with regular feeding, exercise and grooming, but it will settle happily wherever its owners are. Mine have stayed in many hotel rooms and small apartments and – although I live in the country with lots of space – where is my Leo? Under my desk at my feet, of course!

There is one thing to consider if you do live in a smaller house, and that is, if you buy one Leonberger, it won't be long before you want another!

A deep bark for uninvited guests.

2 Origin and History of the Breed

There are many variations on what is thought to be the exact origin of the Leonberger, and record keeping and translation problems result in some areas of contention. The most favoured explanation of the origin and development of the breed is given below.

Heinrich Essig of Leonberg

Heinrich Essig lived from 1809 to 1889 in the small town of Leonberg, Wuttenberg, Germany. Leonberg is situated about 10km (6 miles) from

'Herr Friedrich's Berghund, Moulon.'

Stuttgart. Mr Essig was one of the most important and well-respected people in the town. He sat on the council, and was also a great animal lover and enjoyed dog breeding. It was his idea to try to breed a dog that looked like the lion on the town's crest, an idea that later proved very popular and created a high demand for the breed amongst the aristocracy and other more wealthy citizens.

Essig started some very interesting crossing of breeds and close in-breeding. According to Jockers, who wrote his dissertation for the Institut fur Tierzucht, Verebungs–und Konstitutionsforschung der Universitat Munchen, his first mating was between a St Bernard dog and a Landseer bitch. He then crossed the progeny for four generations.

'An ideal type.'

The results of these early matings are thought to have been mainly black and white spotted dogs about the size of a St Bernard. Essig then acquired a new, more yellow-and-white St Bernard dog from the St Bernard monks, in exchange for which he gave them two of its progeny.

Essig had a very handsome Pyrenean dog and, as white dogs were very much in fashion, he tried to breed a predominantly white dog. The matings resulted in a colour that some say was silver–grey and others white, but with the black mask associated with today's Leonbergers. These dogs were an immediate success.

It is from these original matings that the dog acquired the liveliness and ability to swim of the Newfoundland; the strength, loyalty, tracking ability, body and good nature of the St Bernard; and the agility, fine hearing and sight of the Pyrenean. All three breeds are very hardy and can endure cold and damp.

In keeping with fashion, Essig placed great importance on the colour of the dog. Over the years the colour developed from black–and–white to black–white–red, and thence to the colours we know today: red–brown, gold–yellow and, in particular, the lion–gold, all with a black mask. In 1865, however, a Leipzig paper reported that 'many are snow white with black noses and dark eyes, some are white with black masks, some have a few black patches and, very occasionally, ones which are all black', so it seems that it took a long time to establish the colour. Essig soon began to export his 'breed', and in an 1860's paper is a paragraph about a lady from Philadelphia, USA, called Miss Wellesley, who had purchased a Leonberger. It is described as having an intelligent black head with yellow coat.

The first true Leonberger is said to have been produced in 1846, and with it the first German town to be associated with a breed of dog. The citizens of Leonberg had an obvious pride in the breed. For many years, while owners of other breeds paid a dog licence, the Leonberger was exempt. It is also thought that for some time the car licence plates had a small head of a Leonberger on them as well as the number of the car.

The fine, lion-like breed soon became very fashionable, so much so that it is said that the following prominent people had them: Richard Wagner, Bismark,

Napoleon III of France, the Prince of Wales who later became Edward VII, King Umberto of Italy and Garibaldi. The Empress Elisabeth of Austria owned seven, one of which was described in an Austrian paper as being silver-grey and as having cost 1400 silvergulden in 1870. It is said that Essig sent 374 dogs to Russia in 1873 and a further 325 followed in 1874. Two were sent to the Suez Canal in 1869, insured for 400 gulden. The Mikado of Japan kept Leonbergers in his palaces and it is thought possible that they lent their blood to the modern Japanese Tosa.

In 1857, two Leonbergers went to the St Gottard Pass where they fulfilled their duties quite as well as the 'Barry Dogs'. (Barry was another name given to the St Bernard's.) Sadly, the prior of St Bernard wrote to say they had died in 1868.

It is thought that the first registration by a breeder, that is, the date of birth and particulars of the dog given, was recorded by the Prior of the St Bernard Hospice. The original registration is in the museum in Bern.

Three German painters, Spech, Leuitemann and Beckmann, painted pictures of Essig's breed.

'The ideal Leonberger, 1895.'

The breed went from strength to strength during Essig's lifetime, but when he died the critics made themselves heard. In 1905, a Herr Strebel published a book on *German Breeds and their Ancestry* with observations on all breeds. Strebel gives a short history of the Leonberger but fails to mention the Pyrenean outcross. It seems that Strebel found them quite nice dogs but, although undoubtedly recognisable as Leonbergers, simply an outcrossed St Bernard.

Vero Shaw's *Book of the Dog* had three pages on the breed. There is no publishing date but it must have come out shortly after the Battersea Dogs'

Home was built as plans for the home are included in it. Perhaps Strebel was influenced by Shaw's book, because here also is the claim that the Leonbergers are nothing but poor specimens of the St Bernard breed. The very first paragraph tells us that the breed is a mixture of breeds and really has no place in a book on dogs, but that the editors included it rather as a warning than to laud its merits! Vero Shaw is also reputed to have said that the Leonberger is nothing more than a giant mongrel.

'Minka' on an early French postcard.

In 1878, Herr von Schmiedeberg is quoted as saying, among other things, that only in the opinion of the breeder and a few low dealers was the Leonberger a valuable breed. Almost the whole of the second page in *The Book of the Dog* is taken up by Schmiedeberg in an attack against Essig and his breed.

At least one German came to Essig's support. Mr Charles Goas claimed that when an avalanche wiped out the dogs at the monastery, Essig, who had two St Bernards, immediately responded to the tragedy and offered his two animals to the Hospice. Before they left he made the experiment of crossing them with his Newfoundlands, not over a few years as Schmiedeberg claims, but over a long time, to produce the Leonberger breed.

From *The Complete Newfoundland* by Margaret Booth Chern (1975) comes the following quotation:

Herr Essig owned both Newfoundlands and St. Bernards and inter-bred them. It is claimed by Hubbard that Essig added crosses from Swiss Mountain Dogs, Wallis Sheep Dogs, Kuvaszok and either Austrian Jadggriffons or the Bavarian Geburgsschweisshune. Harvey claims that only the three progenitors mentioned by Jockers were used. A more startling claim comes from H C Brooke that he (Brooke) owned a common European wolf bitch which mated freely with his dogs and he sold a number of these hybrid pups to a dog dealer in Leonberg. It has been further claimed that these powerful hybrids were successfully used in the creation of the Leonberg dog. Here let us consider coat colours of the Leonberg dog. Although today blue-grey and fawn are prevalent, at one time black, black–and–white and wolf-grey occurred frequently.

Chapter 2

Fiona Karolus, one of the first people to bring Leonbergers into the United Kingdom, and to whom I am indebted for the help in collating the history of the breed, disputes Margaret Booth Chern's claim that today blue-grey is a prevalent colour in Leonbergers. Fiona travelled extensively in Germany visiting breeders between 1971 and 1973 and attended Leonberger shows at the town of Leonberg. She says, 'nowhere did I see a blue-grey specimen though some were more liberally tipped by black on the hairs of their coats so as to appear darker than the golden dogs most desired. Their basic colour was some form of red, red-brown-yellow, fawn or golden-yellow.' She goes on to say that Margaret Booth Chern's claim that at one time black, black-and-white, and silver-grey did appear is not disputed, but not in the seventies. Perhaps Margaret only saw puppies, which are born silver-grey!

A number of sources confirm that Leonbergers were introduced into Newfoundland and at one time may have threatened to oust the native breed. In 1902, a newspaper quoted that 'Newfoundlands have become so scarce in their own country that the British government has lately been obliged to purchase for Newfoundland lifesaving stations a new breed of dog to take their places. These are Leonbergers, a cross between Newfoundlands, St Bernards and Pyreneans. They are the most powerfully built dogs in the world and stand more than four feet high. Those sent to Newfoundland the British government paid from 250 to 400 dollars and some sold for as much as 500 dollars'.

For the Leonberger to be quoted as 'four feet high' (1.2m) leaves us in a quandary. If the writer meant the dog was this tall when standing on its hind legs, then in this case it would seem that the dog was quite small by today's standards, as most modern dogs would measure between 1.5-1.8m (5-6ft). Perhaps it was a simple misprint, or maybe the writer was using poetic licence!

A family pet in 1935.

In the 1890s a club formed in Apolda in Thuringen. Later, it was named the Leonberger Club and had its seat at Heidelberg, moving yet again to Stuttgart and finally to Leonberg. In 1895, Albert Kull wrote the first standard. In 1922, Herrs Stadlemann and Josenhans reformed the club with a few others who had managed to keep their animals alive. With around five dogs, which became the foundation animals, they built up the population of the Leonbergers, and are largely to thank for the Leonbergers that we know today.

Within four years, these gentlemen had raised the numbers to 350, and the first stud book was kept from 1922. However a few pedigrees have turned up dated prior to this. Take, for instance, Marko vd Kochlinsmuhle. He must have been put to a bitch in 1919, but his own pedigree and breeder are unknown. He was mated to a bitch named Bella three times, as far as we can

The Leonberger in 1939.

ascertain, but the results of these matings are unknown. We do know, however, that he had three sons and these were used at stud: Friwo 11 von Kochlinsmuhle whose line died after six generations; Friwo v Oberhausen whose line died after

A Leonberger bitch in 1955.

three generations; and Marko v Neukirch, born 2 November 1920, bred by Herr Winz of Rottweil. This line continued.

During World War II the breed was almost wiped out, but it survived thanks to the work of Albert Kienze and Otto Lehmann. A new club was formed in 1948 with its seat, most fittingly, in Leonberg.

Mrs M Lertmann-Blusshenstein, a member of the German club, and her dog in 1956.

Five litters were recorded in 1945 and 14 dogs and 8 bitches were registered. From here the breed grew very slowly with only 2132 dogs and bitches registered with the German club from 1945 to 1970.

One of the founder members of the German club was Edith Kraus who was the first person to register a kennel name, von Pappelhof, with the club. Frau Kraus died in the late seventies. Another founder member was Robert Beutesbacher who bred one of the foremost dogs in the breed, Carlo von Glemstal. This dog is said to have fathered over 50 litters, and most of today's dogs feature him somewhere in their pedigree. Another breeder whose dogs have influenced the breed greatly is Frau Muller who uses the prefix v Murrtal.

According to Nelly Leonard, who writes in the United Kingdom stud book, after the Second World War a German kennel named von Rossbach mated a black Newfoundland bitch to a Leonberger dog, and this lineage can be traced in many German pedigrees even now.

The Austrian Connection

Another theory of the origin of the Leonberger was put forward by the late Professor Dr von Schulmuth, who discovered from his researches into various private family journals that the breed was known in Austria in the district of Wolfberg as early as 1585, if not before. In a journal dated 1601, belonging to the Metternich family who lived near Wolfberg, are entries showing that they owned Leonberger-type dogs on their estates for many years to guard against cattle and sheep thieves.

To add weight to this theory, Mademoiselle de Geineste from Courivause, Marne in France says that an ancestor of hers, the Marquis de Pluival, was a page at the court of Marie Antoinette. The queen brought with her from Austria some dogs described as 'very fine'. These were known by the same name, Leonbergers, but were more commonly called the Chien de la Reine. The Marquis liked these dogs immensely, and was honoured when the queen presented him with some to take to his home. From that time the family have always kept this type of dog, and can trace their ancestry back to those first dogs. Mademoiselle de Geineste owned a miniature painting of one of her ancestors, which included a Leonberger. Sadly, this was lost during the Second World War.

According to the findings of Professor von Schulmuth it was the dogs belonging the Imperial family of Austria that were the starting point for the Metternich family, as they were used on the country estates as guards for the Imperial family in the 16th century. Dogs of this type often appear in old paintings.

Leonbergers were quite commonly seen working in Lorraine, Flanders, Wurttemberg, Bavaria and villages in Austria in the 1800s. They were used to pull carts, either singly or in pairs. Those found working in Flanders and Lorraine often had Bouvier blood in them, and only those used for exhibition purposes were considered pure bred.

Winter 1956. The Leonberger in its role as draught dog.

The origins of the name under this theory therefore must show a different light. Perhaps the first part, 'Leon', was given because of the dog's resemblance to the lion, and 'berg' because of the mountain connection. Or perhaps 'berg' was tacked on from the original district of origin, Wolfberg.

3 The Modern Leonberger

At the present time, there are approximately 18–20,000 Leonbergers world-wide, but the number is growing as the popularity of this noble breed increases. The Leo even has its own pages on the World Wide Web. Yes, Leos are on Internet, with a lively correspondence address where Leo enthusiasts from all over the world can maintain contact. Type in the word 'Leonberger' on your search program and see how much Leonberger information is at your fingertips. This information is updated all the time.

Xilja von Crumelbach of Glanzberg (left) and Zingo von Bernerland (right), the first two Leonbergers to come from Switzerland in 1979.

Leonbergers in Britain

The earliest report of a Leonberger in England is in 1865, when a Leonberger took first prize at a show, but it was not until the early 1950s that two more were brought into the country by a couple of servicemen returning from Germany. In 1974, Fiona Karolus brought in Catja v Tannenheim, a bitch in whelp. Unfortunately the bitch died during the birth and the puppies with her. In 1975 Mr and Mrs Nealing imported Dixi von Engelhof and in 1977 the same couple imported Assia vd Sieben, both from Germany, but no Leonberger progeny resulted.

Also in 1977, Sonia Gorbould found a pair of Leonbergers in Switzerland, Zingo von Bernerland (Graf) and Xilja von Crumelbach of Glanzberg (Leonie).

She arranged to bring them to England in partnership with Fiona Karolus and Celia Peters. When they came out of quarantine in 1978, Celia Peters (now known for the kennel name Rossnick), took Leonie and Fiona had Graf. It was soon apparent that Graf was unhappy on his own and so Fiona sold her share in him to Celia and the dogs were reunited. Tragically, Graf died soon after of stomach torsion.

The next dog to come into the country was Chatkantara Adkin of Rossnick (Boyka). Boyka sired the first litter of six pups to be born in the United Kingdom. There were four bitches and two dogs, one of which (Amea) was exported to the United States.

Rossnick Can Indeed (Pepsi). International Norwegian and Swedish Champion. Owned by Kari Woldmo of Norway.

Late in 1980 two more Leos were imported from the kennel of Wanda Oud in Holland. Lady Anamar of Pelgrims Ring went to Sue Carmen and Lady Bronwyn of Pelgrims Ring joined Celia Peters. Lady Bronwyn went on to produce the Rossnick 'C' litter of which one puppy, Rossnick Can Indeed (Pepsi), was exported to Norway and became Norway/Sweden International Champion.

The next import, in 1982, was Sir Faramir Fuego of Pelgrims Ring (Lutz) (see page 22). He belonged to a partnership between Celia Peters and Angela Bursill.

Many more new dogs were imported, and enthusiasts of bloodlines and pedigrees should consult the stud book. Perhaps one of the best known of more recent years is the dog imported by John Feehan, Leonberget'z Crusader from Atlantis (Jabba). He went on to sire Manorguard Adam who, as we go to print, is this country's top winning dog.

Sir Faramir Fuego of Pelgrims Ring (Lutz).

British Leonberger history really began to be recorded with the very first club show held on 1 July 1990 at Kinghern Kennels, Basingstoke, Hampshire. The judge was Sonia Gorbould and the entry exceeded expectations, with 59 dogs entered making 150 entries in the breed classes and 28 entries in Obedience.

Leonberget'z Crusader from Atlantis (Jabba), father of Manorguard Adam.
Photograph by Diane Pearce.

Norwegian and Swedish champion Normanscourt Alfred of Rossnick (Alf).
Bred by Sue Carmen.

Sonia's comments at the start of her report stated, 'a lovely well run show, happy friendly atmosphere, and some first class Leonbergers'. She went on to say, 'To be super critical, you could do with a bit more body and bone on a lot of the dogs. Heads could do with some improvement, most dogs are quite close behind, and I also had a lot of variation in colour.'

Best in Show was awarded to Celia Peters with Norwegian and Swedish Champion Normanscourt Alfred of Rossnick (Alf). The week before this, Alf had taken Best of Breed at Blackpool Championship Show. Sonia Gorbould described him as 'superb, a fine specimen of a Leonberger'.

Best Opposite Sex, Reserve Best in Show, First Post Graduate Bitch, went to Miss Bate and Tesal Bestinay The Nedni of Lawndown (Jocheena). She had won two classes at Crufts 1990, Special Yearling and Post Graduate Bitch, and went on to win Reserve in Any Variety Not Separately Classified.

Best Puppy in Show went to Mr Fred Inwood and Puppy Dog Katchino v d Hexenbrucke of Kinghern (Bertie). Bertie was only ten days out of quarantine. Bertie is brother to Kassandra vd Hexenbruke (Heidi), and the two of them were the first dogs to be exported to Great Britain from Germany (see page 24).

Other major placings were:

Puppy Bitch: Mr and Mrs Thomas's Devinco's Witch of Endor (8 months old).
Junior Dog: Mrs Morton's Rossnick Ee-By-Gum.
Junior Bitch: Mrs Stillwell's Gildasan Eine Kleine Nacht.
Beginners: Mr and Mrs Thomas's Gildasan The Gambler.
Novice Dog and Post Graduate Dog: Fred Inwood's Gildasan My Boy Arkle.
Open Bitch: Celia Peters' Lady Libra of Rossnick.
Veteran: Larry Rahmer's Besimee of Rossnick.
Stud Dog: Angela Bursill's Sir Faramir Fuego of Pelgrims Ring at Rossnick.
Brood Bitch: Celia Peters' Flickan Fiasco.

Three levels of Obedience were judged by Peter Marchant. Pre-Beginners and Beginners were won by Ann Newman with Jancarby Moonbeam (Sasha), and Novice was won by Joan McLennan with Flickan Fireball of Glenkham (Chalie).

The show also attracted a guest from Belgium. Nelly Leonard, a very experienced exhibitor and breeder of Leonbergers, was asked to do her own critique from the ringside.

In 1991, Eric Van Duin from Holland officiated as judge and kindly and most constructively gave his comments for places for all to hear. Eric's wife, Wanda Oud, accompanied him and

Bertie and Heidi, the day they came out of quarantine in June 1990. Ten days later Bertie won best puppy at the Leo club show.

made her assessment of the dogs. (Incidentally, all of Eric's top-winning dogs also gained top ratings from Wanda.)

Best in Show: Jenny Hamilton-Jackson's Flickan Firefly At Montanes.
Best Opposite Sex: Juliette Morton's Rossnick Ee-By-Gum.
Best Puppy: Christine Gapp's Rossnick Happy as Larry.
Best Opposite Sex: Rossnick Hocus Pocus, sister to Happy as Larry.

In the Obedience section, judge Pat Langridge awarded Pre-Beginners to Margaret Beeley and Jancarby Moonrocket. Both Beginners and Novice were won by Ann Newman and Jancarby Moonbeam of Coombevalley, sister to Moonrocket.

Open bitch winner, Celia Peters' Lady Libra of Rossnick.

The show has continued to gain momentum over the years and is always well attended. Judging by reports from judges and assessors, there are some excellent Leos to be seen.

The Kennel Club has classified the Leonberger in the Utility group. Many breeders and owners are unhappy with this, as the Leonberger has great potential as a working dog. The dilemma for The Kennel Club is that there is already the similar-looking Estrella in the working group, and the working group already poses logistical difficulties at shows due to its massive size. Perhaps in the future this could be rectified with the addition of a separate group for herding breeds, as in other countries. I would add that in the historical papers the Leonberger is described as a 'utility dog' because of the various ways it was capable of working with man.

As Leonbergers have developed, there are a few 'Leo firsts' worthy of mention. Alf (Normanscourt Alfred of Rossnick), owned by Celia Peters, was the first Leonberger to win the Best Unclassified at Crufts and go on to be judged in the Utility group. The first Leonberger to win the Utility group was Mr Fred

Inwood's Arkle (Gildasan My Boy Arkle at Jancarby), at the Crystal Palace open show under judge Stuart Mallard. Arkle (see page 27) enjoyed an illustrious show career, taking another Leo first when he became Best of Breed at Crufts 1991, the first year classes were scheduled there for the breed.

At the present time, the highest place attained by a Leonberger in this country goes to John Feehan and Glenda Smith's Manorguard Adam who, handled by Glenda, took Best of Breed, and went on to take the reserve best in the Utility group at Crufts 1995. He was best Rare Breed in 1995, has won over 80 Best of Breeds, several Best in Group at championship shows, and has sired many show-winning pups. Both his parents, Leonberget'z Crusader from Atlantis at Manorguard and Leonberget'z Lady in Red at Manorguard, were imported from Sweden by John Feehan. His father (Jabba) was

Manorguard Adam, who has achieved the highest honours in the United Kingdom to date, seen here becoming Reserve in the Utility group at Crufts 1995. Owned by John Feehan and Glenda Smith.

previously the highest-winning dog, following his achievements at Crufts 1992 and 1993, where he made the last six in the Utility group judging.

Leonbergers in America

The Leonberger has been imported into America successfully since 1971 but is still considered a rare breed. After the war, the first Leos were introduced by Keri Cambell. During the 1980s several breeders imported dogs and set up breeding programmes, each oblivious of the others' attempts.

The Leonberger Club of America (LCA) was formed in 1985. It maintains a register of all the Leonbergers in America, and now just over 1000 dogs are registered.

The LCA has spent many years establishing breeding criteria to ensure that the breed is not ruined by greed, carelessness, irresponsibility, poor breeding programmes and lack of knowledge. The Club maintains the only official International Leonberger Union and German-recognised register of Leonberger dogs in the USA. Only puppies that have been bred according to the LCA's strict breeding regulations can be registered officially. The LCA recommends that prospective purchasers should buy only from breeders approved by the LCA.

The International Leonberger Union

Because of the increase of awareness and the spread of the breed around many countries, the Union of Leonbergers was formed. Member clubs include: Germany, Belgium, Finland, France, Sweden, Norway, Italy, Great Britain, Denmark, Netherlands, Spain, Switzerland, Austria, Czech Republic, Slovakia, and the United States of America. No doubt other countries will join as the breed spreads around the world and its popularity increases.

150 Years Celebration of Leonbergers

At the end of May 1996, Leonberger enthusiasts from around the world gathered at Leonberg, near Stuttgart, Germany, to exchange gifts of friendship and to enjoy a weekend of mutual celebrations for 150 years of Leonbergers.

Superb Leonbergers from around Europe paraded on stage at a special party to acknowledge some of the achievements. The next day, almost 300 Leonbergers were entered in a show held at the Club's own premises.

The first Leonberger to win The Kennel Club's Utility group, Fred Inwood's Gildasan My Boy Arkle at Jancarby (Arkle).

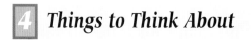

4 Things to Think About

Long before you get your Leonberger puppy there are many things that you should consider. Many of the following points apply to any breed, but the Leonberger does have a few idiosyncrasies.

Floor Surfaces

It is important to think about the environment that the pup is coming into. A slippery floor is not good, as the pup will slide around. This can affect the dog's construction, because it cannot walk correctly, and therefore its bones and joints are unable to form in the right way. Its feet suffer and it may end up with permanently splayed feet instead of the wonderful 'catlike' paws that it should display.

Stairs or steep steps are another problem for growing pups, but especially for larger breeds like the Leo. Constant use of stairs puts unwanted pressure on its growing joints.

Puppies and Water

Leonberger pups love water, but this can have its drawbacks if you are house

A cat litter tray makes an ideal first Leo pool.

Later, you can progress to something a little deeper.

proud. Dogs have no concept of mud and cannot comprehend the human dislike of it in the house. I have yet to find the Leo that checks its paws before entering the house and parading on the best Axminster or Wilton. Therefore, it is in everyone's interests that you provide an area where your Leo can have access to water without access to areas that matter. Mine have a large tub in the garden, but for very young pups a cat litter tray is an ideal and inexpensive starter tub. It is easy for them to get in and out of and is quite safe. As they grow you can increase the size and depth if you wish. To my mind, there is nothing more pleasurable than watching a Leo messing about in water, but if your Leo becomes an addict (as many do), it is a good idea to put this behaviour under command so that you are not dragged into any water your Leo spots.

Exercise and Leo Pups

Many people who have never owned big dogs automatically assume that such animals need lots of exercise. This is true to a degree but, when the pup is very young, exercise should be restricted to as much as it wants to do itself. Free play with another dog is acceptable, as long as that other dog does not continue to pester the pup after it has had enough. Walks need to be built up very gradually, in speed, distance and frequency. Your Leo will be at least 18 months old before it can cope with any endurance walks, and then only if you have maintained a gradual build-up for stamina and fitness.

Young Leos need limited, controlled exercise. Photograph by Pam Wells/Travelling Light

Slow, short rambles are better for the growing pup. It will probably trot along, alternating spurts of speed with sections taken at a slower pace. If it can have some safe off-lead walks, all the better. These help it to develop socially because it can investigate new things at its own speed. Woodlands, heathland with streams, and safe rock pools on the coast are all excellent exploring grounds for growing minds and bodies.

Avoid becoming a creature of habit. Try to think of different routes for your regular outings, or at least stop en route for games and training sessions at random. Always make it fun to be out together. Explore with your Leo, don't just leave it to investigate alone, and you lay the foundation for a great life together. If you leave it to do everything on its own, you teach it that you are not interested. When it goes off on its own at inappropriate times later, you will have only yourself to blame.

Worming

Your breeder should give you details of when and with what your pup has been treated against roundworm. This is not the end of the worming. You need to continue to follow the course and worm your pup with either the same preparation or one prescribed by your vet. Make sure that what you use is suitable for puppies and weigh your pup to make sure you give the correct dosage. Follow the instructions on the packet. Once it is over 12 months, your Leo should be wormed every six months, or more frequently if you suspect an infestation.

Inoculations

From a behavioural point of view, seven weeks of age is the optimum time for a pup to go to its new home. At this age your pup has not normally been

Six-week-old Scout (Akamai Amigo).

vaccinated, although it has gained a certain amount of immunity to disease from its mother. At eight weeks you need to take it to the veterinary surgeon for a course of inoculations. The inoculation will need to be boosted every year or as appropriate to circumstances in your area.

You will be advised by the vet to keep your Leonberger pup in until it has had all its inoculations. At this age a puppy is very vulnerable to diseases passed by other dogs. During this time you can take your dog out, but you must be sensible about where you take it. Choose places where other dogs do not go, or where you know that the dogs are free from disease and have not been in contact with other animals that might not be so well protected. Rides in the car, visits to friends, a beach as the tide goes out leaving clean sand are good places to take your pup. I am sure you can think of more clean, safe areas where your pup can socialise and learn about the big, wide world. Avoid built-up or highly-populated areas, areas where dogs run free, parks, and so on. It is important that socialisation is carried out during this time if your Leo is to be well adjusted, so please do not take the vet literally when he says the dog should be kept in. The object is to protect against disease, not to isolate completely.

During this time of relative confinement, you can start some basic control training and get the dog used to its lead and collar. Before you get to the stage where you want to take the pup for a 'proper' walk, you must teach it how to walk on a lead and show it that this is a pleasant activity. Do this in the garden and in the house before attempting it in a new environment (see Chapter 12, Basic Training).

Puppy Classes

It is a great idea to take your pup along to classes, but it is essential that you are sure of the class and its ethics before you start. Always go along and have a look before taking your dog. If everyone is having a good time and the dogs are under

Learning about the world is tiring! Sumo, photographed by Pam Wells/Travelling Light

Do not protect your pup from the outside world. Photograph by Pam Wells/Travelling Light

control without a lot of shouting (or worse) going on, then it is probably a good class. Avoid going to classes where confusion seems to be the order of the day and owners are being advised to use pincher collars. choke chains or aggression towards their dogs. Some classes do not seem to give advice at all, and leave problem dogs in corners, telling everyone to give them a wide berth.

Your Leo can be trained easily on a leather buckled collar and lead or, at the most, a half check collar or slip lead. It does not need anything more harsh. So start as you mean to go on, and find a good dog school that has a motivational, behavioural approach to dog training and socialisation.

You and your Breeder

Keep your breeder informed at regular intervals of your Leo's progress, both good and bad. All breeders are interested to know how things are going and love to see photographs now and again. It will be of great benefit to the breeder and the breed in general for you to get your Leo's hips checked, and have any other tests that are appropriate at the time (even if you do not wish to breed from your dog yourself). This data can be entered into the records and help breeders to make more informed decisions for future breeding programmes. It would be wrong of you to hide, or neglect to tell your breeder of, any genetic defects that may show themselves later, even though he/she may not be happy to hear of them.

If at any time you decide to change your Leonberger's circumstances, always refer back to your breeder and purchase contract first.

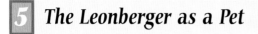

5 The Leonberger as a Pet

Leos in the Home

Leos are home-loving creatures. Saffi relaxes on the hearth.

Leonbergers are 'people' dogs, that is, they thrive in an environment where they can be part of the family. They take exception to being isolated and, if left alone for long periods without being given an otherwise full life, suffer stress which can lead to physical and mental trauma.

The fact that they are home-loving creatures does not mean that they can never be kennelled, in fact, quite the contrary. They love being outside and enjoy lying out in the fresh air. On a summer's day they actively seek out cool concrete, shade and, if possible, water. If you do have to leave your Leo for relatively long periods, it is kinder to allow it the freedom of an outdoor life, preferably with a companion. The environment should be secure and in an area that protects your Leo from being interfered with by strangers. A large enclosure is best with an area of natural shade, and a shelter to allow the dog to get away from heat or harsh weather. Most Leo enthusiasts adapt part of their garden or yard to allow their dogs freedom and security in this way.

If you intend to give your Leo a companion, I must stress it is best not to have two puppies at the same time. Puppies are very time-consuming and you need time to train and build up a relationship with your dog. If you have two at the same time, the dogs will naturally bond together. This is not always a good thing as they will look to each other instead of you at important times, so training becomes difficult.

Taking on any dog is a large responsibility, and you must be sure that you have the time to attend to all the dog's needs. If you and all the family have to be away from home all day, having a dog is not really advisable, and expect problems if you do take one on. Most responsible breeders do not sell a puppy if they think that the prospective owner is not in a position to care for all the dog's needs.

The Leonberger serves as a good guard. Its deep bark and sheer size are enough to warn off uninvited guests. It is always a good move to put the bark under command. Invited guests are always welcomed by the well-socialised Leo but, if you fail to teach your Leo the social graces, it may not react in the desired manner and you could end up losing your friends. Many Leos enjoy escorting their family and friends into the home by gently holding an arm or a piece of loose clothing. Most owners allow this rather touching behaviour. If you find it a problem, it easy to train out by teaching the 'leave' command and rewarding the desired behaviour.

Some lines of Leos have a predisposition to be more dominant than others, but it is not always easy to determine whether a pup is going to become dominant. Dominance is in-born, but you can do much to keep it under control. It is more prevalent in male dogs, but females are not immune. It is a good idea for any Leonberger owner to read up about dominance and to follow at least some of the rules to be sure of keeping control.

Leos are water-loving animals, and often this means that they drink their water messily. Be prepared for your Leo to drink, or rather spread, large quantities around your kitchen floor. Most Leo owners have a mop permanently situated next to the water bowl.

It is tempting to take two puppies, but it is best to wait until one is older and has learnt the rules before introducing another.

Shamoo proving that Leos love the water. Photograph by Pam Wells/Travelling Light

Leos have heavy coats, and some moult a lot. Most have a yearly or two-yearly moult, and the rest of the year hair loss is down to a minimum. Much depends on the climate and temperature in which the Leo lives. Excess heat will result in more loss of coat. Leos who spend much time outside, particularly those adults who sleep out-of-doors or somewhere very cool, usually have heavier, more profuse coats.

Leos and Children

Children love Leos – Leos love children. It seems a perfect partnership. However, both Leos and children need to learn the rules of living in harmony. It is best to involve the children as you train and socialise your Leo, so that they can learn the skills as you go along. Even very young children can help in the training, with an adult firmly but kindly backing up their actions.

Leos love children but, like Tyson, need to learn the rules.

It is always tempting for children to roll around on the floor with fluffy, cuddly dogs. A rough-and-tumble with the teddy bear Leonberger is great fun but it is better to discourage this behaviour. It is very easy for the Leo to perceive the lowering of body posture as a submissive gesture. This is all very well until the child attempts to assert some dominance over the dog, which takes exception to it. All of a sudden, the dog is a threat or even an aggressive, not-to-be-trusted dog, when really it was just being a dog. You may also find that your Leo attempts to mount a child that is accessible in this way. When this first happens most children laugh or think it is all part of the game. However, once the Leo has started this behaviour it is self-motivating, and often becomes a problem. It is more common in adolescent males, but even females do it sometimes, and can be either purely a behavioural problem or linked to hormone imbalance. It is best to avoid these sorts of problems by not allowing children to take a lower level than the dog, and certainly you should never leave young children with any dog, whatever its breed, and however stable you may think its character is. Never forget that it is a dog and not a differently-shaped human.

Children must be closely supervised if they are allowed control of your Leo – like this 'wet set' posing for the camera.

At some time most children will want to take the Leonberger for a walk. Once again this should be done only under adult supervision. The powerful Leo could quite easily pull a child over. Many Leos are very calm and it is easy to feel that the child will be safe, as indeed he may well be, but do not take unnecessary risks.

The Leo is an excellent family pet; the children will adore it. Just make sure that your heart does not rule your head so that you allow or overlook potential dangers.

Taking on an Older Leo

If you are thinking of taking on an older Leo, you should be aware of potential problems. These would apply to any dog, not just Leos, but with a Leo comes power and strength which, if not under control, have potential danger for all concerned. If you are a competent trainer and are aware of or accustomed to the size and strength of the dog, you should be able to conquer any problems, and life can be most enjoyable for both you and the dog.

Most Leos that come up for re-homing (and I must say it is quite rare) are available because there is some part of their behaviour that is unacceptable to their present owners. Occasionally, you may find a very well-trained Leo available because it has not made the grade in the show ring or is unsuitable for breeding, or perhaps changed family circumstances force a reluctant parting. Whatever the reason, there is work ahead for the new owner, as in many respects the dog must be cared for like a puppy. It must be taught the ground rules of your home, introduced to its new surroundings and walks, and make friends with any other animals and family members. You must constantly ensure that you are fully prepared for any problems.

Bringing an adult dog into a household of other animals is rarely an easy matter. If you have other adult dogs, particularly of the same sex, you should give the matter careful thought. Unless the dogs have an easy-going, placid acceptance of other dogs, they are unlikely to accept a newcomer without incident. Ideally, the initial contact should be on neutral ground and, if at all possible, they should meet a few times and have time to get to know each other before being thrust together in your home. In practice this is rarely possible, so you should plan to introduce a new dog to your home at a time when you are going to be available to monitor and control its progress, at least until it settles in and finds its own level.

Male Leonbergers are usually more difficult to get to accept each other, as often they develop strong tendencies towards dominance. It is important to assess the status of each animal, both prior to and during integration, to try to identify which will be the more dominant so that you can back the top (alpha) animal and help to maintain the hierarchy. In so doing you should never undermine your own position as 'top dog', and ultimate control must rest with you. You must be prepared to intervene and put both dogs in their place if necessary.

Backing the alpha animal means feeding it first, showing attention to it first, allowing it to do things before the other dog and so on. It is very tempting to favour the underling but, if you do this, you will boost its conception of its position and elevate it so that it is more likely to pick a fight – a fight that it will probably lose. Do it a favour, and keep it where it belongs.

Having said that dogs are more difficult, bitches are less pliable and, once they decide that they do not like another bitch, it may be very difficult to persuade them otherwise. Bitches have more possessive natures than dogs and a serious fight is much more likely to occur following a trivial argument over a toy or bone. Fights amongst bitches are often more severe than those between male dogs.

Introducing an adult dog of the opposite sex is usually the easiest option from a behavioural point of view, but of course brings its own problems if the animals are not neutered.

New dogs should not be introduced at times of heightened awareness, for instance, when a bitch has puppies, or where there is already a male and female and the female is in season. Of course it is common sense not to introduce new dogs if one of yours is ill; even if the illness is not contagious, the suffering dog will not feel at its best to make new associations.

Having prepared you for the worst, it has to be said that in general Leos get on well together, and in many cases new dogs can be carefully introduced with great success.

Occasionally the situation is just too traumatic and liable to cause distress and/or injury to both dogs and owner. In this case you will have to resign yourself either not to take the dog on, or to keep the dogs separate for much, if not all, of the time.

6 *The Show Leonberger*

The show standard is a set of guidelines agreed by The Kennel Club and the Leonberger Club as a standard by which to judge the Leonberger. The standard can be changed, but any changes should always have the furtherment of the dog's best interest at heart.

The Leonberger Show Standard

By definition a good show specimen should be very sound and of good temperament fitting to the breed. In order to move correctly in the ring the Leonberger's conformation has to be good, although poor Leos can win where Leo classes at shows are ill-attended, or when an inexperienced judge is captivated by an individual or, worse, influenced by a handler.

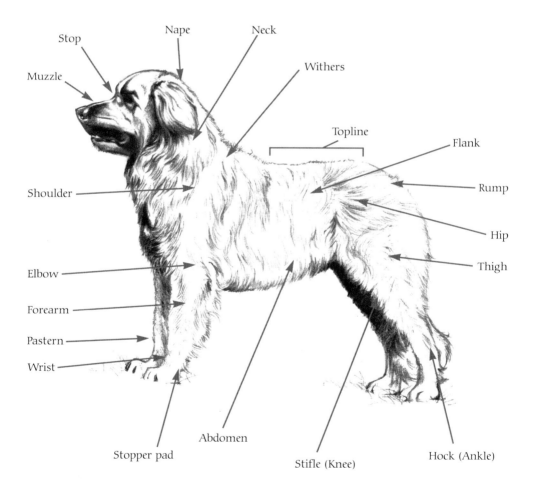

Points of the dog

World Champion Dreigon vd Hexenbruke. Owned by Herr W Gullix of Germany.

The Kennel Club Standard

General Appearance Strong and muscular.
Characteristics Faithful, intelligent, amenable, good watch dog. Web-footed.
Temperament Equable, self-confident, neither timid nor aggressive.

Eik von Haus Schluter following his win as Best in Show, Norway, 1992.

Head and Skull Tolerably wide skull; moderately deep. Broad, not too short, square muzzle. Slight stop, no wrinkles.

Eyes Medium size, dark and intelligent, good natured expression; showing no haw (the third eyelid or membrane in the inner corner of the eye).

Ears Set on high, close to head and not too far back. Wide as long, rounded at tip, well feathered and pendant.

Mouth Lips black and well-fitting with no open corners. Jaws strong with a perfect, regular and complete scissor bite, ie, the upper teeth closely overlapping the lower teeth and set square to the jaws.

Neck Strong, moderately long. No dewlap (loose skin under throat).

Forequarters Shoulders well laid, elbows close to the chest; forelegs straight and well boned.

Body Slightly longer than height at withers. Strong back and loins, chest deep, ribs well sprung but not barrelled.

Hindquarters Strong and muscular. Hind legs angulated and parallel when viewed from behind. Hind dew claws removed.

Feet Tight, rounded and webbed. Pads black. See diagrams below.

Tail Well furnished, carried at half mast, never too high or over the back (see diagram on page 44).

Gait/Movement Strong and firm.

Coat Medium soft to hard, fairly long, lying close to body despite good undercoat. Slightly wavy but never curled. Very evident mane to throat and chest on male dogs.

Colour Light yellow, golden to red-brown, preferably with black mask. Dark or even black points permissible. Small white star on chest and white hair on toes permissible. Hair at throat, on forelegs and underside of tail may be brighter.

Size Height at withers: Dogs 72–80cm (28.5–31.5in); Bitches 65–75cm (25.5–29.5in).

Faults Any departure from the foregoing points should be considered a fault and the seriousness with which the fault is regarded should be in exact proportion to the degree.

Note Male animals should have two apparently normal testicles fully descended into the scrotum.

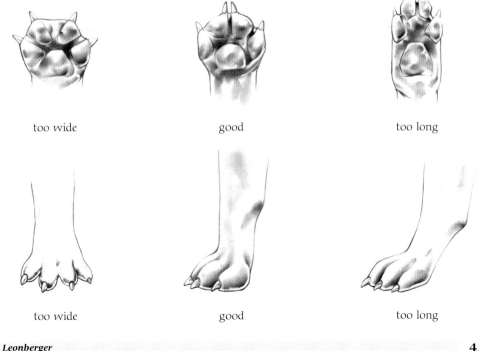

too wide	good	too long

| too wide | good | too long |

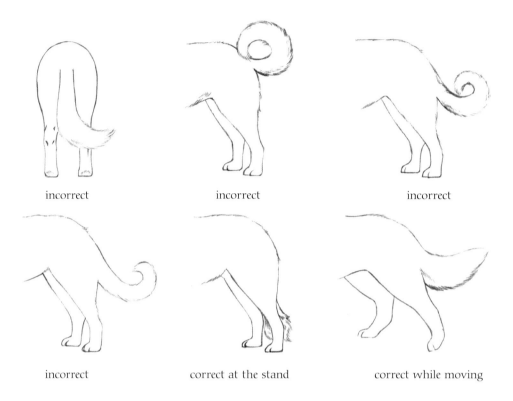

incorrect   incorrect   incorrect

incorrect   correct at the stand   correct while moving

Show Breeders' Notes

While researching this book I had the opportunity to speak to some of the top show breeders, judges and handlers in the United Kingdom and Europe. The following are some of the pointers and guidelines that they use to assess a good show-quality dog, but still adhering to The Kennel Club standard.

General Appearance Males should exude masculinity, females should be feminine whilst still fitting the criteria of strong and muscular. There should be a very obvious difference between male and female that is evident without checking genitals. Powerful and elegant, impressive and noble.

Characteristics Capable of a day's work, but also happy to lie around relaxing with the family. Weather-proof and water-loving.

Temperament Calm but

Maritima Borgeus Amirz at 10 weeks...

... and as a fully-grown, adult male.

lively. Sometimes slightly aloof with strangers but never aggressive.

Head and Skull   Not heavy like a Newfoundland, more equal and balanced. Head carried proudly. Occiput not distinct. Length of muzzle equal to the top of the skull. Moderate sloping stop.

Eyes   Kind, calm, tranquil expression. Slightly oval (almond shape). Preferably dark, definitely not yellow. Size in harmony with the head.

Ears   Size should be in proportion to head. More triangular than round.   Head should give the appearance of being flat across the top – ears set in line and close to the head.

Mouth   Black flews (upper lips) and dark gums. Teeth full dentition – 42 teeth, good and strong. Drooling is a fault, jowls and flews should be tight to avoid this.

Nose   Large and dark.

Aspen, with the yellow collar, was born in the United States as a result of artificial insemination. His sire is Leonberget'z Crusader from Atlantis at Manorguard (Jabba), Best of Breed at Crufts 1992 and 1993. His dam is Champion Koko Con Der Hexenrose.

Pups getting together at a show, gaining valuable social training from an early age.

Aspen, the day he won his rare breed championship.

Neck To give a balanced elegant look. Powerful, blending into shoulders.

Forequarters Shoulders: angulation well laid back. Straight and parallel from shoulder to ground when viewed from the front. Elbows point to rear. Pasterns strong and slightly sloping to allow flexibility.

Body Depth of chest should come to elbow and be two thirds of the body. Topline firm, straight and balanced. Double coupling, that is, good length between last rib and front of pelvic bones.

Hindquarters Powerful, well-muscled. Stifle is moderately angulated, hock to ground – line perpendicular. Front and rear angulation in proportion.

Aspen as an adolescent, and rather an ugly duckling.

Feet Cat/lion-like. Webbed, pads of feet black.

Tail Length at least to hock. Set to follow natural line of the croup. Carried straight down when relaxed. Slightly higher carriage with a modicum of curl is allowable when excited. Well feathered and bushy.

Gait/movement Cat like (walk like a lion), regal, strong, elegant and balanced gait. Strong drive showing effortless power. No signs of swinging or arching in fore or hind legs.

Coat Weatherproof, unbroken mask is preferable, ideally extending over the eyes. Feathering on fore and hind legs and ears, and underside of body and tail can be lighter in colour than body of dog, but must blend in.

Colour Light sand to lion gold, red to rich mahogany. Black tips allowable on the outer coat.

Size Within KC criteria – balanced.

Faults Absence of mask. Brown nose or pads. Black and tan, Black, Silver. Too much white (star bigger than palm of hand on chest, extending from toes to middle of foot, white in other areas). Curly or very wavy coat. Too light an eye. Loose eyelids. Loss of pigmentation on flews. Hocks which turn in on each other (cow hocks). Roach backed (dip towards the loin). Insufficient angulation. Turned out feet. Under- or overshot. Curled or carried high tail. Entropian and Ectropian eyes. Shy or aggressive. Also, of course, any deviation from the standard.

Glenda Smith (seen here at Crufts) adjusts Manorguard Adam's posture to give a balanced 'four square' stand.

Adjust the gait speed to produce a graceful stride.

Selecting a Puppy for the Show Ring

Selecting a puppy for a specific purpose is never easy. Even experienced breeders get it wrong more often than they would like. If it were so easy, breeders would have all the top dogs, and the lesser specimens would be put into pet homes.

Most puppies are selected by their new owners at the tender age of six or seven weeks, and it is best from a behavioural point of view if they can be on their way to their new homes around the seventh week. Of course, from the show point of view, it would be better if the pups were allowed to develop a little more before choosing the perfect specimen, but waiting for the time when the Leonberger's body shape can be determined would mean waiting perhaps 18 months. Many of our top-winning dogs, if seen at six months old, would not win anything. At some point in their physical development almost all Leonbergers go through a rather leggy or uneven stage – sometimes the back end higher than the front, sometimes the other way around.

To select a pup for the show ring you need to place it on a non-slip table and assess the various points. Scaled down, you are looking for the pup to fit the criteria given in the breed standard and, by using the show breeders' notes, after a bit of practice you should be able to see the good and bad points of the puppy. It is a good idea to see as many pups as possible; most breeders are only too pleased to show off their puppies to interested parties, and to make the best of the visit for socialising the pups. Follow this through and assess the dogs once they are mature. This exercise will stand you in good stead, and increase your ability to pick out the good from the mediocre.

In some smaller, faster-maturing breeds, breeders can have a good idea if a pup will make the grade for the show ring by six months. Unfortunately for the dog, often this means that breeders hang on to potential show dogs, which means that they miss out on important social training in the new home. It is never easy catching up, and often almost impossible for the dog to reach its full potential. Thankfully, in Leonbergers this practice is rare, as hanging on to several big puppies brings its own logistical problems and most breeders are pleased to take their chances on selection at around seven weeks of age.

Preparing for the Show Ring

Whatever the age of your Leonberger, it is a good idea to make a start on training straight away. It might seem an impossible task to teach such a young pup to show, but start as you mean to go on and showing will become second nature to both of you.

In all countries where Leonbergers are shown, it is not necessary or desirable to put your dog into an unnatural pose. In some countries it is frowned upon to correct your dog's position in the ring, but teaching it to come naturally into a 'four square' stand and to look alert will aid your chances in the show ring in any country.

Standing 'four square' means that the dog looks balanced and shows to its best advantage. Its legs are parallel and straight, its feet point towards the front, and its overall appearance is not hunched up. Training for this means that the dog comes into position easily and naturally without you having to manipulate it into the correct position. Dogs of good conformation tend to take up a four-square posture quite naturally, but to have it under your control means that you have the optimum chance of making it look outstanding when it matters. Also practising the perfect gait makes sure that you and your dog are in harmony in the ring. To those regularly attending at the show ring, it is obvious whether or not a handler has trained him/herself and the dog in preparation for the day.

Even with a dog the size of a Leo, the initial puppy training is often best done on a table or other suitable surface. Make sure the pup's feet do not slip by providing a piece of carpet or rubber matting.

Lift the pup up on to the table. At first it may be a little nervous but, with gentle reassurance and a positive attitude from you, it will soon become confident. When it has settled down, raise it into the stand position, putting your left hand under its tummy for support, and have a titbit in your right hand, held so that the pup has to reach for it with its head up. You want to teach it to stand still, so keep a firm hold of the titbit. Do not reward the pup if it moves forward, sideways or backwards. Only release the titbit when it is standing still.

Once the pup has mastered standing still, you can start to position the legs so that it learns to stand four square. Go to each foot in turn, making sure that it is facing the front until the legs are standing apart and parallel. Then start to touch the pup, sliding your hands all over its body as a judge would, not forgetting to open the mouth gently to expose the teeth. All the time you are doing this, repeat the word that you are going to use for the show stand: 'Stand' or 'Show'. If you are teaching other disciplines such as Obedience, it is a good idea to have a different word for the stand in each instance.

'Gait' is the term given to describe the dog's pace. It is important to practise this as well as the stand. With a young pup it is simply a matter of getting it used to the lead, and then encouraging it to trot at your side, slightly away from your body and with its head held high. Encourage this by using toys or titbits. Also it is worth experimenting with collars and collar position. Sometimes a collar held high around the neck helps to give the dog lift, but this looks false with other dogs which may be better shown on a loose lead.

As the pup develops you need to adjust the gait speed to show the dog to its best potential, and remember that you are aiming for a graceful stride. Road walking and trotting at the side of a bicycle help to build up muscle and enhance your Leo's gait. Remember not to overdo the exercise while your Leo is growing.

Most people show Leos on a fabric or leather slip collar and lead or a half-check collar and leather lead. The collar and lead need not be heavy or wide, as this will be too cumbersome in your hands; a 1.25cm (0.5in) wide lead and collar is ample.

Grooming and Bathing

Some Leo owners rarely bath their dogs, whilst others always have a bathing session before a show. Whatever the situation, a well-groomed dog showing a healthy coat, with neat nails and clean ears never goes unnoticed in the show ring. In some countries you are not expected to trim any hair from your dog, in others it is common practice to trim hair from underneath the pads and to tidy any hair growing between the toes. Trimming hair from between the pads helps to prevent the feet from splaying.

If you want to bath your Leo before a show, do this two or three days in advance to allow the coat to settle. A high-powered dryer is a good investment, as the dense coat takes a long time to dry, and the dryer does tend to give it a good finish.

A good time to bath your Leo is after it has moulted. A good-quality shampoo gets rid of the dry, flaky skin that tends to appear during the moult. When your Leo is out of coat, a bath and blow dry will make it look and feel a lot better.

It is important to groom your Leo thoroughly before bathing it as any dead hair mats, and matted hair tightens when it is wet. You will know that the dog is completely groomed when you can comb down to the skin and see the skin clearly anywhere that you part the hair. Many owners make the mistake of surface grooming, thus leaving dead hair underneath. This can become irritating for the dog, and will lead to overheating in the hot weather.

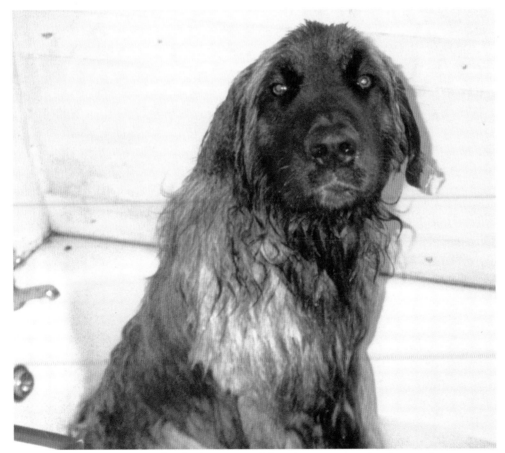

Leos love water, but bath water and shampoo are not quite the same!
Alamo prepares for Crufts.

7 The Working Leonberger

The Leonberger is a very versatile breed of dog, capable of turning its talents to a multitude of activities. There are many benefits in taking up dog sports for both you and your Leo. The activities allow it to use its natural talents and help keep its mind active and channelled in the right direction, its body fit, and it may even increase your chances of winning at the breed show – a well-muscled dog always looks better in the show ring.

The Working Section of the Leonberger Club of Great Britain was set up by Lee and Lesley Gray in 1994, following the first official character assessment of a group of Leonbergers by Mr Graham Mabutt, who is well known for his talents in assessing working ability and character of adult dogs. Mr Mabutt was adamant that the Leonberger had tremendous potential and should be looked upon as a working dog.

Tsagan demonstrating a five-person pull. Not part of a formal test, but very impressive nevertheless.

Lee and Lesley, being Newfoundland as well as Leo owners, first set out to explore the area of water rescue. They joined a club to train both breeds. To their surprise, the Newfoundland refused to swim, but their Leonberger, Tsagan, took to the water straight away and they never looked back. Other Leonberger owners and their dogs soon joined in the fun.

In 1995, the Leonbergers were invited to take part in a public display of water rescue work at Grangewaters in Essex. Four Leonbergers and five Newfoundlands gave three separate performances to a large and delighted crowd as part of the annual Festival of Watersports. Various other displays have been given by the Leonberger Working Dog Section at events around the country and Leonbergers are now doing well in draught work such as Carting, Agility, Obedience, Flyball and Nosework as well as Waterwork, some at competition level and many others just for fun.

The Leonberger has been used for a wide variety of tasks around the world. There are reports of Leos being used in search and rescue, disaster work, flock guarding, hunting, police work, aids to the disabled, and so on, as well as taking part in hobby pursuits such as backpacking.

The Leonberger truly is a most versatile breed.

Odin works with his owner, John Anders, caring for and controlling wild deer.

Waterwork

Some countries have a special pre-water test, called the tadpole test, which is non-competitive and fun. This involves a simple fetch; a dunk (the dog retrieves a toy or article that sits just below the surface of the water); the send (the dog retrieves a boat bumper or retrieving dummy from a steward who is in the water). The dog handler and dog get into the boat which is then pushed into the water, and an oarsman takes them out for about a minute. The oarsman returns to shore and the dog must remain in the boat for a few seconds under relative control until the judge announces the end of the exercise. For the swim, your dog is held by a steward on the shore, you swim out around 7.6m (25ft), the dog is released and swims out to you and then you swim back to shore together. Once you start entering competitions you can progress through various levels of competence.

Waterwork enthusiasts are a very relaxed bunch of people who help each other and are happy to progress slowly. If you are interested in doing Waterwork with your Leonberger, join up with a group that can help you to

Learning the basics – being enticed around the handler, and then taking the toy back to the bank.

The boat tow.

learn the all-important aspects of safety in the water, as well as the training techniques of Waterwork. To find out where these groups are, contact your nearest Leonberger Club or, if you do not have a local group, often Newfoundland Clubs will let you join in their sessions.

The Leonberger Club of Great Britain Working Section follows the Newfoundland Club rules for Waterwork and their official certificates are awarded to qualifying dogs.

In one end ...

Agility

Agility is a fast-growing sport that made its debut at the Crufts dog show in 1979. The Leonberger is not associated instantly with Agility, but in fact it is very good at this event, quickly mastering the obstacles with the help of its power and working ability. However, a Leo is not known for great speed in this event, and is hard pressed to keep up with some of the more agile breeds. This does not deter many Leonberger owners from having a great time and picking up some prizes along the way. A fit Leonberger, with a lean, well-muscled body, can

Leos love Agility. Joan Mclennan's Chailey (Flickan Fireball of Glenkhan) in competition at Ardingly in the United Kingdom.

work at the same level and speed as any German Shepherd.

Bonnie Goodfriend of the United States is possibly the best-known Leo/Agility fan and is noted as the first person to have an Agility-titled Leonberger in her dog, Frieda. Bonnie says that Frieda gets faster and faster each

... and out the other. Linda Raynor's Kaiser, photographed by Pam Martins.

time she competes, and her confidence soars. To watch Frieda run an agility course is to see beauty and grace in motion, and she often brings the watching crowd to their feet.

Leos in Germany demonstrating their obedience under trainer Harry Peffer.

Obedience

Obedience is, of course, an important part of your Leonberger's character as without obedience it will be very difficult to handle. In this context, however, obedience has a capital 'O', in that I am talking about Competitive Obedience.

In the United Kingdom, Obedience is a very competitive sport demanding a high degree of accuracy. It can be compared to dressage in the equine field. Unlike Border Collies, working sheepdogs and German Shepherds, Leonbergers are not a common sight in the open or championship Obedience competition ring but, on the occasions when they do appear, they certainly turn some heads. Their graceful yet powerful gait makes a good performance mouth-watering to say the least but, as with any sport, much preparation is necessary before the dog is ready to compete and win at this level. Handlers compete against each other for top awards, and at championship level the competition is extremely tough. Many Leonberger handlers are starting to take Competitive Obedience more seriously and I am sure we will see a United Kingdom Leonberger Obedience Champion at some time in the future.

In other countries, dogs and handlers do not compete against each other, but towards a standard for qualification. This gives the Leonberger as much a chance as any other breed to qualify.

Working Trials

In Great Britain, Working Trials is a sport in which Leonbergers can really excel. Few are actually competing regularly at the moment, which I feel is a great shame.

The only drawback with Working Trials is that it is quite a time-consuming sport. Individual trials are often run over several days, and training itself involves preparation and the search for and use of clean land for the scent work.

The tests are made up of a combination of: nose work (tracking and searching), steadiness to gunshot, speak (bark) on command, agility and obedience. At the top level there is also a class for police dog work.

In Working Trials, the dog is working to qualify rather than competing against the rest of the entrants, and this gives the Leonberger the opportunity to qualify amongst the best.

Flyball

Flyball has been popular in America and Canada for some time, and is a fast-developing sport in the United Kingdom. In 1996, the only known Leonberger competing at Grand Prix Flyball competitive level was Liz Guy-Halkes' Eersteen. Of course there are many more enjoying the fun of Flyball at club level who, no doubt, will join in at the competitive level at some future date.

Eersteen, the United Kingdom Leo Flyball champion, shows his paces during a competition. Owned and trained by Liz Guy-Halkes.

Schutzhund

Once again this an area in which Leonbergers can excel. It involves criminal work and obedience, and has many similarities to the British Working Trials. Shutzhund is a sport that has its roots in Germany, but is gradually spreading around the world.

Working tests in Germany.

Draught Work

When the breed was in its infancy, it is likely that it was used by the ordinary person to pull carts for bakers, butchers, the dairy and various other activities.

For modern Leonbergers, draught work is more likely to be seen in competition, or used by the hobbyist. Although many people may have ideas of progressing the Leo's usefulness in this area, it is not legal (at least in the United Kingdom) to use any dog for the purpose of drawing or even helping to draw a cart or truck on a public highway. Therefore any draught work in which you employ your dog must be on private land, even if it is part of a demonstration. The laws may be different elsewhere and it is advisable to check before venturing out with your Leo.

Competitions as well as demonstrations of draught work are developing into a great sport, with all levels of standardised draught tests, starting with easy courses that progress to more complicated and exciting feats.

Learning to pull with a simple log pull.

Then on to a cart

Join a local training group which is experienced as well as sympathetic to the dog's needs. If you cannot find a local Leo group, try the Bernese Mountain Dog or Newfoundland clubs, as these often work together with Leonberger owners.

Special Duties

Therapy Dogs

Leonbergers have some very special attributes and one of these is an uncanny and very natural ability to work with people who are unwell or in need of special care. The Leonberger's role as a therapy dog is both exciting and gratifying. Many owners are astounded as their Leo changes attitude and posture when meeting small children, the infirm or people with special needs.

Of course it is most important that your Leo is of stable character and has undergone a good training and socialisation programme before embarking on therapy work but, once trained, it is wonderful to see people enjoying your dog.

Qualified therapy dogs go into hospitals, old people's homes, special schools and, in fact, anywhere else where they are requested. They bring great joy to those who may, because of their circumstances, be unable to have dogs of their own.

Tsagan demonstrates the ultimate in pulling with owner Lee Gray.

Blood Donors

There is always a desperate need for canine blood donors. The Leonberger, being a large dog, is an ideal candidate for inclusion on the blood donors' list. A placid dog that sits still and relaxes whilst blood is taken is ideal for these duties.

Special Dogs

Some Leos, like Juliet Morton's Igor pictured right, excel in their special duties. Igor is a registered PAT (Pets as Therapy) dog,

Igor, blood donor, PAT dog, and carer of the orphans.

having made his first visit at the tender age of ten months. He attends numerous sessions, helping with talks to scout groups and old people's homes, and has been

Misty (Lowengolds Natalia) as lead sled dog.

regularly reported by the media. He is also involved in Juliet's rescue work, helping with kittens, puppies, baby goats, chickens and donkeys, amongst others. Igor is also a blood donor, helping to save the lives of many dogs.

There are many more Leos around like Igor, who have that something special which makes them perfect for this sort of work. I am sure that I could fill a book with the numerous special Leonbergers around the world; perhaps someday someone will.

My own Willow has many special duties. She accompanies me when I teach and acts as a demonstration dog. She comes along to book signings and trade shows to meet the public and her attractive looks and personality act as a inducement for those who are shy, because few people are able to resist running their hands through Leo fur. She works with students who are learning handling techniques, patiently accepting their mistakes, as well as being an angel with children with special needs. Willow's son, Scout, is just starting to learn the ropes, and soon he will accompany me as well.

The author's Willow, meeting the public at a book signing.

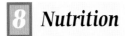

Good nutrition shows on the outside as well. Photograph by Pam Wells/Travelling Light

Nowadays, puppies are weaned onto a complete and balanced meal which can be bought from pet shops. Many major feed companies manufacture a range of foods specifically designed for the various lifestages of the dog. The largest companies spend a lot of time and money researching and carrying out field trials to perfect these foods. Therefore it makes sense – particularly considering our busy lives – to make good use of this expertise and feed a ready-prepared diet.

Some breeders prepare their own diets, but they are becoming relatively few and far between. Still others use a combination of prepared and home-made diets.

If you are happy with the condition of your pup when you buy it, there is no reason to change its diet from one brand to another. In fact, this can have detrimental effects on the pup's well-being, both from a physical and psychological point of view. If you do not have the expertise or the time to prepare a home-cooked diet, it is better to transfer your pup gradually to a ready-prepared diet, and thus you will ensure that it has everything it needs. At least for the first few days, however, try to stick to the breeder's régime. If anyone advises you to change the brand of food, please think carefully before doing so. Sometimes certain brands of food are wrongly accused of causing upset stomachs. Even veterinary surgeons have been known to advise new owners to change to a particular brand that they stock. If the pup is fed a good-quality puppy food by the breeder, and does not have an upset stomach when you collect it, it is highly unlikely to be the food that causes the problems.

Changes in diet should be made very gradually. Often Leonbergers have smaller appetites than you might expect for such large dogs, and you may mistake the fact that the dog does not need vast amounts for lack of interest. The best guideline for quantity is to feed as much as the pup can eat in 10–15 minutes and then take up any uneaten food. If body weight looks good (not too fat, not too thin), and the pup is progressing well, then there is no need to worry. Let the pup be your guide rather than the text books or feed guides.

Pups should be maintained on a good (premium) brand of puppy food for as long as recommended on the packet, which usually is until they are five or six months old. They can then progress to a junior version of the food. This is maintained until approximately 18 months to two years, by which time the pups can transfer to the adult version. All brands differ slightly in their cut-off points between puppy and adult, but you should bear in mind that your Leonberger cannot be classed as adult until it is at least 18 months to two years old. With some, it is obvious that they are not fully developed until they are three years old, so choose a brand of food that takes account of this.

Pups enjoy food moistened with warm water or puppy milk. To aid digestion the food is best served moistened, but occasionally pups enjoy

Feed the pups on a good-quality puppy food.

crunching it in the dry format. Do not feed ordinary cow's milk as this has no nutritional value to dogs. Use only bitch milk substitute or goat's milk. Even older dogs benefit from better digestion if their food has been soaked in warm water for a few minutes.

New developments in nutrition mean that several brands of puppy food are now available specifically designed for large breeds. It will be interesting to see the results of these new foods, because the true outcome can never be known until they have served at least one generation and its progeny.

Leonbergers of all ages need good quality nutrition.

Some breeders believe that Leonbergers should not be given high-protein diets like those found in many of the premium products; others recommend that Leos be taken off the puppy diet as early as four months but more usually six months, changing to a moderate adult diet at this time. Yet again, others have successfully reared their Leos on the whole selection of lifestage products.

It is obvious that more research is needed in the field of large, fast-growing dogs and diet. For new owners, the best course is to compare all the available information, and make a decision based on this and your breeder's and vet's advice.

When it goes into its new home, the pup suffers stress and trauma. It has left the only family it has ever known, and often there are no other dogs or animals that it can relate to. Everything is foreign. It is rather like you being thrust into a foreign country, unable to speak the language or communicate effectively in any other way, with no family or friends to relate to, and everything new and confusing. Quite a daunting prospect, isn't it? It would be nice if at least the food remained the same!

Your pup might have felt ill on the journey, which will make it think that its problems are caused by the last thing it ate. If this happens, do not worry unduly. Let your pup settle down and become accustomed to its new home for a few hours. Try offering some puppy milk later; the pup is more likely to take some of this than solids if it is feeling ill, and at least then you know it has something in its tummy. Next, mix some milk with a little puppy food, leave it to soften and feed it in a sloppy consistency. It won't be long before your Leo pup regains its appetite. Give it only food that it is used to from the breeder unless absolutely necessary, as changes in diet will upset its tummy more.

If the pup develops loose motions or other upsets, do not blame the food if you have continued as above. If the pup was not loose when it left the litter, it cannot be the food that is causing the problems. Look for other causes. Stress, excitement, and bacteria and viruses can all cause your pup to develop loose motions and sickness.

Contact your veterinary surgeon if the puppy is in distress or any symptoms last for more than 12 hours without showing signs of improvement.

Water and Leonbergers

Leos don't always realise what is for drinking and what is for playing in!

Always make sure there is plenty of fresh cold water available. Leonbergers do drink quite a lot, and often enjoy playing in water, especially when the weather is hot. It might be a good idea to supply your pup with a low tray of water to play and cool off in (outside, of course), as well as its drinking water. Later you could purchase a dog bath for this purpose. Unfortunately, it is not easy to tell your Leo which water is for playing in and which is for drinking, so you should always make sure that both lots of water are clean enough to drink.

How Many Meals?

Assuming your pup comes to you when it is seven or eight weeks of age, it will need four meals evenly spread throughout the day. As it grows and develops, gradually increase the quantity given, guided by the pup's weight and appetite to maintain good condition. You may find your pup reluctant to eat if the weather is hot, but don't worry, offer the food later in the day when it is cooler.

Feed to condition rather than worrying about recommended portions.

You will probably find that the pup is less keen to eat one of the four meals after about a month, so allow this meal to drop when the pup is ready. Your Leo pup may be about a year old before it shows signs of not needing the third meal. Once again, be guided by your pup's weight and condition rather than text books and feeding guides.

Some breeds of dog thrive on just one meal a day when they reach maturity, but it is best to feed a Leonberger twice a day for life. This is because it is a large breed and cannot utilise the volume of food efficiently all in one go.

Weight Control

In common with many other large breeds, Leonbergers have a low base metabolism, and many do not eat as much as you might expect. Therefore it is best to feed to condition rather than worrying about exact amounts.

Overweight

If your pup starts to become too heavy, this could cause permanent damage to its growing limbs. You should be able to feel the pup's ribs easily, without them being prominent. Keep a close eye on its growth and adjust the food intake accordingly. Any treats should be counted in as part of the diet. Avoid treats containing sugar. The best titbit to use in training is part of the meal.

When your Leo becomes an adult exactly the same applies. It is relatively easy to maintain good weight and condition by keeping a close eye on your dog. Simply cutting down on food to get weight loss is not always the answer. Leos do need good-quality exercise to keep their muscles in trim. They need a certain amount of food to maintain the health of the whole body, including internal organs. Therefore look at the whole régime, and reconsider your exercise plan as well as diet if your Leo is overweight or unfit.

Underweight

A dog that is underweight is not always helped simply by being given more food. Often the Leo will refuse to eat the extra amount anyway. If your Leo is underweight, make sure that you are feeding a good-quality premium food that is known to be easily digested. Chicken or lamb-based foods are often best. Develop an exercise plan so that the dog has good-quality exercise to build a healthy appetite and help the body utilise the food correctly.

There can be underlying reasons for lack of weight so it is a good idea to check with your vet if your dog remains underweight for very long and you are unable to correct it, or if the weight loss is sudden.

Supplements, Additives and Extras

Important Do not add any extras to the diet in the form of supplements if the pup is being fed a good-quality, premium balanced diet. Your puppy does not need extra calcium, vitamins, minerals or oils in any form. Puppy foods are scientifically formulated to give the perfect balance. Calcium is an element of the diet that is very important when an animal is growing. Just because the Leonberger is a large breed does not mean that it needs specifically more calcium than other breeds – yes, it does need plenty of food, but in the correct proportions. Additives will upset the balance of prepared foods and could cause long-term physical problems.

If you are feeding a made-up diet then you should study the nutrition books and decide what extras are needed, and your veterinary surgeon can advise in this area.

A feeding stand makes good sense.

Feeding off the Ground

It is advisable to feed your Leonberger at head level, rather than allow it to reach down to the ground. This is because all deep-chested dogs are prone to a condition known as torsion (see Chapter 9). Feeding at head level helps to prevent this. You can make your own make-shift feed stands from up-turned boxes or buckets, or you can buy proper feed stands at dog shows and specialist pet shops.

Feeding Behaviour

Poor Appetite

Some Leonbergers have what many people would class as poor appetites, and many owners tempt their Leos with 'little extras'. This is not really good practice unless the 'extras' are part of the dog's normal food ration. Appetisers should not be given separately, as feeding titbits for no reason promotes reluctance to eat normal meals.

I have found that, in many cases, poor appetite is a result of too much food being given at a time, or poor management of intake. As I said earlier, Leonbergers have low base metabolism, which means that they do not need to eat as much as you might think. Another reason for poor appetite is low activity

Activity levels make a difference to amounts of food needed.
Willow the Leo – and Leo the Border Collie!

levels. Some Leonberger owners do not encourage their dogs to be active, so the dogs tend to spend many hours sleeping. When awake, many Leonbergers do not see the need to rush themselves or repeat actions, unlike some other breeds. My Leos eat only marginally more than my Border Collies, and when you see them playing together it is quite obvious why. The Border Collie, even if left on its own, will play with its ball for hours, while the Leos play for a few minutes, spend a few more minutes strolling around majestically, and then find a nice cool place for a snooze. Meanwhile, the Collie is still charging around the garden, burning up calories, in pursuit of its ball!

In some cases, dogs have poor eating behaviour because they are low-ranking, submissive animals. This can cause them not to want to eat in the presence of higher-ranking animals (this sometimes includes humans), and at worst they can be extremely difficult to feed to a good condition.

To improve eating habits Feed in an area that is quiet and free from distractions. Reduce your Leo's overall intake by volume but feed morning and evening. Remove any food that is uneaten after 15 minutes, and take note of how much is left so that you can adjust the amount next time. Keep reducing the amount until your Leo eagerly eats all that it is given and then, over a period of days, gradually increase it until you reach a good balance between volume given and desire to eat. Make sure that your Leo is not finding food elsewhere or being given table scraps. Picking at food, even small amounts, throughout the day does lessen appetite.

If your Leo turns away from food occasionally, do not worry. Simply take the food away and offer a smaller meal next time.

Feeding in the presence of other animals (even if it is only the cat) gives competition and so heightens the desire to eat.

If your Leo has been particularly active you need to raise the amount of food. Do not worry if you overdo it; you can always reduce the size of the portion until you get it right.

If your Leo is low ranking it is important to give it its own space and time so that it can relax and not feel pressured. Once it has wound down a little, it will be more inclined to eat. Scientists have proved through studies of stress that low-ranking, submissive animals are in continuous trauma, causing high blood pressure and raised heart rate, and it can lead also to pathological problems.

If your Leo has a poor appetite and is losing weight and condition, or the poor appetite is unusual for your Leo, then seek advice from your veterinary surgeon.

Greedy Leos

Greedy Leos are less common than poor eaters, but they do occur. Here you must be sensible about the amount that is fed and feed to

More food, please!

condition. Greedy Leos finish off any uneaten food left by other pets, and will scavenge. Therefore, you need to be very diligent and make sure that you are fully aware of your Leo's eating habits all the time.

A quality food is essential, and two meals a day give your Leo a better chance of utilising the food that it is given.

Make sure that your worming procedure is carried out effectively, as the presence of worms can cause increased appetite as well. If the increase in appetite is sudden you should think about any changes in care that may have caused it, and also consult your vet.

Teach your Leo to 'leave' on command.

Aggression over Food

It is important with any dog to make sure that its feeding behaviour is acceptable. With a big dog like a Leonberger, do not allow bad manners or you could have problems on your hands. Read Chapter 12: you should make sure that you can approach your dog at any time while it is eating. You should be able to take its food without it questioning your action. It is a good idea to check this regularly. Putting your hand in your Leo's bowl while it is feeding to add more tasty titbits is an ideal way to show it that when humans interfere it is no big deal – in fact, it might be good. Let the children do this too, so that your Leo does not see children as a threat to its food.

Do not allow your Leo to scrounge from the table while you are eating. If you have not reached the stage where you can tell it to lie down, put it out of the room.

Teach your Leo to 'Leave' on command, (see Chapter 13), so that it can be told to leave food not meant for it. The 'Sit' command will also help so that you can control it until you are ready to put down the food. Do not allow your dog to pull food from your hands, whether or not it is its supper. Always make the dog sit before feeding.

9 *Hereditary Defects and General Health*

Almost every breed has some troublesome hereditary defects, and still more are under investigation or suspicion as to whether or not there is a hereditary factor or predisposition.

There are commonly-used tests for some of the defects and, for some, scoring schemes which give an indication of how bad they are. Understanding these will help you to ask the right questions when buying a Leonberger, whether a puppy or an adult. If you decide to breed from your Leo, you need to understand the procedures so that your chosen stud dog or brood bitch is a suitable match for your dog. You should consult experienced breeders and enthusiasts, and perhaps even a genetics expert to help with hereditary problems specific to the bloodlines that you wish to investigate.

Hip Dysplasia (HD)

Hip Dysplasia (HD) is a polygenic problem, which means that it is inherited as a result of the influence of several genes. There is some evidence that other risk factors are early rapid growth and weight gain, and over feeding, that is, too much protein and too many calories, vitamins and minerals. HD shows as a very shallow acetabulum (hollow which receives the head of the femur) and a small or mis-shapen femoral head.

HD is not always easy to detect. Owners and/or vets may become suspicious when the dog starts to limp or appears weak or clumsy on its hind legs. This can be suspected even before the pups have left the litter and up to three months of age. Between three and 18 months there may be little to see, but dogs may become lame or stiff in the limbs and perhaps be reluctant to exercise. Over 18 months the majority of dogs settle down and muscle builds up to compensate for the weakness. In middle to old age, the dog may become arthritic.

A Leo with Hip Dysplasia may be reluctant to exercise, unlike this lively Leo.

You will help to keep your Leo healthy if you are aware of potential problems.

Depending on the severity of the problem and the dog's ability to deal with it, vets may recommend pain-killing anti-inflammatory drugs coupled with a good balanced diet and moderate exercise.

Surgery may be an option, either to improve stability or, in more severe cases, to remove the head and neck of the femur or even replace the hip. It is important to prevent the HD-affected dog from becoming obese as any extra weight puts more strain on its joints and so increases pain.

The only way to be sure that the condition is Hip Dysplasia and to measure its severity is with a radiograph (X-ray). Seek the help of a veterinary surgeon who has a reputation for specialising in the subject of HD. To find such a vet is not always easy, especially if you live away from the city, and you may have to be prepared to travel. Ask other Leonberger breeders and owners for advice or enquire at your local German Shepherd Dog club, or from other clubs whose breeds are known to suffer from the problem.

One of the reasons for choosing an expert vet is that your dog needs to be X-rayed under an anaesthetic. Also you minimise the chance of the X-rays being rejected as unreadable by the panel. When you take your dog for its X-rays you need to take your Kennel Club registration certificate for identification purposes. The X-ray plates are sent by your vet to the British Veterinary Association (BVA)/Kennel Club panel of scrutineers for scoring. The lowest score per hip is 0, the highest possible is 53. Therefore a perfect hip score would be 0:0, and the worst 53:53. It is not possible to score your Leonberger for HD until it is at least 12 months old, although sometimes vets take X-rays earlier if a severe problem is suspected.

The Leonberger breed has an average score, which is the mean of both hips. This average is adjusted regularly as more scores are taken into account. Your vet or the breed club can give you a copy of all the breeds and their scores so that you can compare the Leonberger against other breeds. If you wish to help eradicate or control the defect you should only breed from animals with below-average scores. Results are published by The Kennel Club in *Kennel Gazette*, and the Leonberger Breed Club and/or stud book should have lists of scored dogs that you could look at and analyse when investigating for breeding or working purposes.

Different countries may have different systems of determining the presence and severity of HD. Some countries are more strict than others, and it is difficult to compare the different scoring systems. In America, Germany and some other countries there is strict and diligent enforcement of the breeding regulations, and dogs are not allowed to be bred from without relevant checks and certificates.

HD is not a problem to be taken lightly. Good breeders strive to use dogs with average or below average scores, but the small size of the genetic pool and other contributory factors may influence breeders to use higher-scoring dogs or borderline cases. This should only be done with great care, for the good of the breed and with full responsibility borne by the breeder for the consequences.

Osteochondritis Dissecans (OCD)

Better known as OCD, this is a malformation of the cartilage between the femur and humerus. Like HD, this is a polygenic defect, that is, it is inherited as a result of several genes. Limping and obvious pain often lead to the assumption that an animal is carrying this defect. The diagnosis is confirmed by X-ray. Often it can be operated on by a specialist vet. Animals with this condition should not be bred from.

Eye Defects

There are many eye defects with various genetic origins. The BVA/Kennel Club/International Sheepdog Society monitor inherited eye disease.

Understanding genetic defects will help you when you choose your Leonberger.

Different diseases are detectable at various ages, and dogs are examined by a member of the eye scheme panel and not by your own vet. Your vet will refer you to your nearest tester.

Although it is not particularly common, some Leos do suffer from cataracts and screening for this is recommended, particularly if the dog is to be bred from or if there is some suspicion of that bloodline. The test is done every year. The examiner puts drops in the dog's eye and, after these have taken effect, looks at the eye. Your dog may be a little worried by the experience, as the tester must get very close to its face and the room is darkened, but most examiners take the time to make friends with the dog first.

Other common defects associated with the eye can be seen without testing. These are Entropion (inward turning of the eye lid), and Ectropion (outward turning of the eye lid). Some lines of Leonbergers are known to carry the genes for Entropion. Entropion and Ectropion can be surgically rectified, but affected animals should not be used for breeding.

Some Leos suffer from droopy or weepy eyes, often termed loose eye. Sometimes this condition is more noticeable when the dog is tired, off colour or even when in moult. This is not a desirable trait, and should be avoided where possible in the breeding programme as there does seem to be a genetic link. Most breeders class this as a minor problem.

Umbilical Hernia

This shows itself as a protrusion of tissue coming through the umbilical ring. You should avoid using stock carrying this defect, but some breeders do not regard it as a major problem and continue to breed from affected animals. Another reason for continued breeding is the small genetic pool, and the almost impossible task of finding completely hernia-free lines.

Often umbilical hernias are left untreated because they do not cause any problem to the dog, although unusually large ones may get caught on undergrowth. Sometimes the vet will advise an early repair to be on the safe side, and occasionally the hernia is repaired even before the dog is weaned, particularly if it is large or covered by very thin membrane.

Do not exercise your Leo just after it has eaten a large meal.

If a female is to be bred from, the hernia can be surgically repaired prior to the mating because carrying the young will put extra pressure on the animal's abdomen. A typical time for getting minor hernias repaired is when the dogs go to be hip X-rayed for scoring. After a while the scar heals and little or no trace can be seen of the operation site.

Another reason for not attending to the repair is that it could be classed by The Kennel Club as altering the animal's conformation. You may experience problems in getting permission from The Kennel Club to show an animal that has been reported as being surgically repaired even though the repair cannot be seen unless the under-belly is exposed.

Some hernias are thought to be the result of an over-zealous bitch biting her pups' umbilical cords during the birthing procedure, and not related to the hereditary factor.

Addison's Disease (Adrenal Hypodrenocorticism)

Addison's Disease is a lesser-known hormonal disease in Leonbergers but it is known to exist in some animals. It is a deficiency of cortisol and aldosterone, which results in loss of appetite, diarrhoea, vomiting and weight loss. The disease can be diagnosed by a blood test and managed well with medication. If undiagnosed, it can be quite serious and even lead to death.

Gastric Dilation/Volvulus Syndrome (GDV)

Also known as Gastric Torsion, Stomach Torsion or Bloat, this is a very serious and life-threatening condition. It occurs mainly in deep-chested breeds like the Leo. Disposition to GDV is probably inherited, but many animals are bred from before it shows itself. It usually occurs after a meal, especially if the meal was large and then followed by exercise. The dog becomes depressed rapidly. It tries to vomit unproductively. The dog may salivate profusely. There is a severe abdominal swelling caused by the food and the gas generated from swallowed air. The swollen stomach presses on the diaphragm and makes breathing difficult. Once distended, the stomach tends to rotate, forming a twist (volvulus). This interferes with the blood supply to the stomach wall and sometimes the spleen, causing the tissue to die if treatment cannot be given quickly. It can also put severe pressure on the *vena cava*, the major artery that supplies blood to the heart.

The moment you have any suspicion of this condition, go straight to the vet who will treat it as an emergency. The vet will decompress the stomach by passing a stomach tube down the oesophagus; sometimes he will pass a catheter into the stomach, or perform a laparotomy by keyhole surgery. In cases where the dog is dying, a wide-gauge hypodermic needle is penetrated into the distended stomach to provide relief. Surgery is then needed to fully decompress the stomach and to return it to its normal position. Sometimes vets anchor the stomach in place surgically. The dog is monitored for any cardiac problems, which can be a complication with this condition, and administered with fluid therapy to help control shock. Shock is a major issue associated with GDV, and many dogs do not survive even though surgery may have been successful. After

24 hours, if all is well, the dog is given small amounts of fluid by mouth. After this, small amounts of food are offered and the condition monitored.

It is very common for dogs to have a recurrence of this condition and these precautions should be followed:

- Raise food bowl to shoulder height to prevent the dog taking in too much air when eating (aerophagia).
- Feed several smaller meals instead of one large meal.
- Ensure that all complete or biscuit meals are well soaked prior to eating.
- Give very little cereal in the diet.
- Make sure your Leo rests for 1–2 hours after eating.

Cryptorchidism and Monorchidism

Some male dogs are born with the condition cryptorchidism, where the testicles do not drop into the scrotum, which should have happened by the time the dog is around 10 months. The cryptorchid dog is prone to tumours in later life. Other animals can be monorchid, which means only one testicle has descended. These conditions are hereditary and you should not attempt to breed from dogs who have either of these conditions.

Eosinophilic Panosteitis

Sometimes known as 'Pano', this problem is rather like 'growing pains'. An otherwise healthy puppy suddenly goes down with pain and there is generalised inflammation of the bones. Where there has been no history of injury Pano can be suspected, especially if the pain seems to switch from one limb to another. The problem is self limiting, in that the pup does not want to overdo things and should not be pushed, so long-term damage should not occur. Many other large breeds suffer from this and it tends to resolve itself as the dog matures.

Sensitivity to Anaesthetic

Some Leonbergers seem to be especially sensitive to anaesthetic, and this should be discussed with your veterinary surgeon if an operation has to be performed.

There are many things that can make a dog more sensitive to anaesthetic which are nothing to do with being a Leonberger. These include heart disease, respiratory disease, decreased liver function and dehydration. Leonbergers, in common with some other giant breeds such as Great Pyrenees and Newfoundlands, have low base metabolism, which also gives them low tolerance to barbiturates. Therefore they need far less anaesthetic than other breeds of comparable weight.

Heart Disease

Heart disease in Leonbergers is not a significant problem. A survey and examination was carried out in the United Kingdom in July 1996 by Joanna Dukes McEwan, BVMS, MVM, MRCVS, a specialist in Veterinary Cardiology, as part of a research project to see if Dilated Cardiomyopathy (DCM) occurs in Leonbergers.

If you walk your Leo regularly in grassland, scrub or woodland, do check it for ticks.

In one day, 33 Leonbergers were tested by auscultation (stethoscope). Thirty of these were passed as normal (91%). Three dogs had heart murmurs (9%). The murmurs were very minor and described as a 1/6 murmur. In two of the dogs the murmurs were at the left base, consistent with a mild aortic (or pulmonic) constriction, or a genuine flow murmur. In the third dog the murmur was more suggestive of blood flowing through diseased valves.

All of the abnormalities were described as 'very mild' and 'not likely to result in progression into heart disease'. Joanna McEwan concluded that, "There was no significant heart disease identified in any of the Leonbergers examined. However, as a cardiologist, I am aware that pulmonic stenosis can occur in the breed, and discussion with Leo owners suggests that there may be other congenital heart disease." She also said that it would be worth while for the Leonberger Club to employ a cardiologist to stethoscope test at shows.

DCM does occur in Leonbergers and appears to have a familial incidence, highly suggestive of an inherited problem, although at the time of writing more information is required. Therefore, it is of value to screen Leonbergers for heart disease prior to breeding.

General Health Problems

Recognising when your Leonberger is off colour is part of being an attentive owner. Little things will tell you if your dog is unwell. Often the first sign of illness in a dog is lack of appetite, followed by lethargy, but for some Leos these symptoms are, or at least seem to be, quite normal. Some Leonbergers do spend long periods sleeping and others do not have great appetites; perhaps there are times when prolonged symptoms that appear to be normal should be looked at in more detail, and veterinary opinion sought. Sometimes Leos eat erratically because we over-estimate how much food they actually need, or perhaps the lethargy is caused by the dog carrying too much weight. A change from the normal character is usually a good indicator, but this is just as likely to be down to a social issue as it is to a physical disorder. In order to make sense of any changes you must really get to know your dog, both physically and mentally.

Sometimes you will know that there is something not quite right with your pet, and yet find it difficult to say precisely what it is. Monitor its behaviour and keep a record of any changes. Don't be afraid to take it to the vet for a check-up straight away if you are concerned. Even if the vet can find nothing wrong at that point, he now has a record of your observations and, if there is an underlying problem, it will help him to detect it in the future. Just as with humans, some illness are very difficult to detect or diagnose. The animal cannot tell you what is wrong so you must learn to understand your Leo's language, which it speaks with its body, its condition, its attitude, behaviour, character, eyes and body stance.

Sometimes small upsets can be treated at home, and minor ailments cleared up with a little basic first aid or medication. But you must be very careful when treating illnesses yourself, as seemingly simple problems may be the outward signs of something more complex. I usually use the rule; if this were my baby, would I take him to the doctor? If the answer is yes, then it's off to the vet.

Common Parasites

Fleas

Probably the most common and most talked about parasite is the humble flea. Surprisingly enough, the cat flea is the flea most commonly found on dogs. The fleas land on your pet and indulge in an orgy of food and sex until they die of

Carry out a regular worming programme on your puppy to keep it healthy.

exhaustion about a week later. They lay their eggs on the dog, but these fall to the ground, into the carpet, into cracks and crevices, or into your dog's bedding, and there they stay until a couple of days later, when they hatch. This is why simply spraying your pet is not enough to eradicate the pest. The larvae feed on organic debris for a week or so, and then spin a cocoon. The pupae hatch at any time from five days to several months later, depending on the conditions, and then seek out a host, and so the cycle starts again. The pupae are almost impossible to spot, and can take on the appearance of whatever environment they are in. Each adult female is capable of laying 500 eggs.

There are various products available that break the flea's life cycle. They are based on flea hormones, and contain a growth regulator which prevents the young developing into adults, so helping you to clear your pet of the dreaded flea.

Some dogs have a flea allergy and extra care must be taken to prevent fleas, especially in the summer months when fleas are most prevalent.

Ticks

Ticks are another problem, especially for those Leonbergers who live in, or are regular visitors to, the countryside. There are several types, but the ones that most commonly attack dogs are the sheep and hedgehog ticks. Ticks are most prevalent in grassland, scrub and woodland. They normally live on cattle, sheep, goats, deer, rodents, and of course dogs and cats, but they also attach themselves to humans.

At first, all you can see is a greyish swelling attached to the animal. Close inspection reveals the legs, as the head is buried in the animal's flesh. Left alone, the tick gulps the blood of its host for days before dropping off. Many of the available sprays guard against ticks, and prevention is better than cure. If your pup, or you for that matter, do get 'spiked' by the tick, do not try to pull it off as you may remove the body but leave the mouth parts to fester in the skin. Some people use a lighted cigarette to burn the tick which makes it let go, but this can be dangerous, especially with a wriggly puppy. The best solution is cotton wool soaked in alcohol, ether or acetone (nail polish remover), dabbed on the offender. Also there is a small, commercially-produced tool that lifts the tick off.

Mites

There are several different types of mites; some burrow into the skin, others live on the surface. If allowed, they live their entire life on their host. All mites cause dermatitis, which sometimes is itchy, sometimes not, depending on the type.

Often the first signs are increased scratching or hair loss around the tips of the ears. If left untreated, this spreads and the areas may become thickened or inflamed. Some of this is caused by the mite and some by the animal's own scratching. Some mites such as *Sarcoptes* can cause scabies in humans so it is important that the matter is attended to straight away. *Sarcoptes scabiei* is the mite that is the most common cause of mange. Suspect this if you see red patches under arm pits and on the inside of the thighs. It often causes bare patches around the eyes and ear flaps. If the condition is not treated it will quickly spread around the body, forming scabs, sores and bare patches throughout the coat. Puppies and young children are most susceptible because their skin is soft, but nobody is safe.

The mite *Cheyletiella* causes a condition often referred to as 'Walking Dandruff', because it causes the production of excess scale. Mites will move on to humans but do not live very long. This condition can be treated with insecticidal shampoo (some vets recommend human anti-dandruff shampoo).

Dermodectic or Follicular mange is caused by the mite *Demodex canis*. This tends to be more common in smooth-coated breeds, and can be detected by its dry scaly effect on the coat, and a 'mousy' smell. The skin tends to become thickened and wrinkled. If untreated, a bacterial infection takes hold and the dog may even die as a result. Normally it is transmitted by a mother to her young, and is not easily transmitted to adult animals. It is a very difficult condition to treat, and veterinary assistance is essential.

Otodectes cynotis is an ear mite that lives in the ear canal. The first signs of this are that the dog rubs and scratches its ear, and there is excess dark-brown, waxy discharge. Sometimes you can see the mites as small, white, moving dots. It is possible that a grass seed caught in the ear or another infection can cause your dog to scratch and rub, so it is always best to check with your vet and receive the correct treatment for your Leo.

Worms

As soon as you get your Leo, check up on worming, firstly by finding out what the breeder or previous owner has already done and, secondly, by obtaining veterinary advice on what to do next, or purchasing the appropriate medication and administering it to your dog. It is very important that your pet is protected against major infestation, and any worms already in its system are eradicated or controlled. The most common worms are discussed below, but obviously there are many more parasites. Always seek veterinary advice if you suspect an infestation, and take precautions by regularly dosing your Leonberger with relevant medication as instructed by your vet.

Round worm *(Toxocara canis)* is the most common worm in dogs. It is a large, fleshy, zoonotic (compound animal) worm. It can cause disease in young pups, so careful control is very important.

Pups are affected even before birth by larvae that pass from the bitch's muscles to the uterus after the 42nd day of pregnancy. They make their way through the liver and lungs and eventually into the pup's small intestine. By the time the pup is about three weeks old, the worms have developed into adults. On top of this, the pup can receive more infection from the mother from the formation of larvae in her milk. This creates a heavy burden on the pup's system, and may stunt its growth. It may have a distended stomach, and vomit or have diarrhoea. In very severe cases, a blockage in the intestine can occur. Pups start to expel the worms at around seven weeks of age and, by the time they are seven months, the adult worms are mostly gone. However it is likely that the pup will ingest some larvae which will go into a state of rest. Adult dogs pass large quantities of worms – several thousand can be found in a minute amount of faeces. The egg is very resilient, and in ideal conditions rests for approximately

14 days while the larvae develops inside. The larvae stays inside the egg until it is eaten by an animal, and can survive for up to two years whilst waiting for a host. If ingested by humans, usually children, in most cases the larvae make their way through the body with no ill effects. Very occasionally, they find their way into the eye which may cause an infection that could become serious, but I must stress that this is very rare.

If the larvae find themselves in a bitch, they rest until she becomes pregnant and then most migrate to infect her puppies. Some remain to infect future litters.

Tapeworms, which can grow up to 45cm (20in), attach themselves to the intestine of their host. Often they are not detected until segments are passed by the animal. The immediate host for the *Dipylidium caninum* tapeworm, the most common, is the flea.

Hook worms are stout, short worms with characteristic hooked heads. They attach their mouth parts to the intestinal mucosa, damage the surface and then eat the damaged material. They can cause loss of weight and anaemia. Larvae may penetrate the skin and cause dermatitis.

Ringworm

In spite of its name, ringworm is not a worm at all. It is recognised by typical round areas of pink, inflamed skin with crusty edges. Sometimes the area is just an irregular bare patch, anywhere in the dog's coat. It is extremely contagious, not only to other animals but also to humans, especially children. Ringworm is caused by a fungus, and spores can live away from a host on trees, gates and upholstery for several years.

Infectious Diseases

Most life-threatening diseases for dogs can be inoculated against, and one of the first things you must do is to take your puppy to the veterinary surgeon to ensure that it is fully protected.

Distemper

Distemper can occur in two ways: the first is very mild and may not even be detected. The pup may go off its food and be depressed. Recovery is good and often the pup is on the mend before you realise it has been ill. The more important condition is acute distemper. The dog has loss of appetite, persistent depression, raised temperature, fever, throat infections, dry cough, discharge from eyes, dehydration, vomiting, diarrhoea and hard and painful nose and pads. Immediate veterinary advice and treatment is required. Distemper is most common in un-inoculated puppies and dogs who have lost their immunity. It is passed in bodily fluids and is also air-borne, so can be transmitted without any physical contact.

Distemper is controlled by inoculation. The first injection is given at about six to eight weeks, followed by a second to complete the protection at 12 weeks of age. Thereafter, a booster each year will help to keep the dog healthy.

Canine Leptospirosis

Leptosirosis is a disease caused by a bacterium called a spirochete. The organism is spread by contaminated urine which recovered animals can excrete for up to a year. Rats and cattle, as well as other dogs, can pass the disease (sometimes known as Weils disease), and humans also are susceptible to it.

The bacteria enter the body through breaks in the skin or mucous membrane, through ingestion and, occasionally, through breeding.

In its worst form, it causes sudden death in young puppies, who often show no previous signs of ill-health. The secondary type shows itself by the pup becoming jaundiced, depressed, feverish, followed by vomiting, diarrhoea with haemorrhages, dehydration, shock, and death within a few hours. The third type makes the dog feverish and depressed. Vomiting occurs with pain and swelling of the kidneys together with halitosis and oral ulceration. The fourth and final type is very minor and often is not diagnosed. It causes fever, depression and lethargy and lasts only a few days.

Vaccines are available to prevent this disease and these are included in your inoculation package when your pup visits the vet. Annual boosting is essential because immunity is short lived.

Canine Parvovirus
This can cause sudden death in puppies, and they show signs of heart failure. Symptoms include vomiting, which degenerates to bile or blood-stained fluid, and profuse liquid, red/brown, foul-smelling diarrhoea. The pup dehydrates rapidly and goes into shock. Death occurs in a very short time if untreated. Once again this disease is preventable by an annual inoculation.

Infectious Canine Hepatitis (ICH)
In its worst form, this can cause sudden death in newly-born puppies. They may be off their food for a short while, and occasionally cry because of abdominal pain. In the acute form, dogs become depressed, feverish and have pale or jaundiced mucus membranes. They have abdominal pain, throat infection, and may pass diarrhoea with blood in it. They may appear tucked up and reluctant to move. The sub-acute form is recognised by depression, loss of appetite, and corneal oedema or 'blue eye'. The virus is excreted in the faeces, urine and saliva, and may continue to be secreted up to six months after the dog has recovered.

Kennel Cough
Kennel Cough, also known as Canine Cough or Canine Bordertella, is brought about by inhalation of micro-organisms and causes a dry cough. Often it sounds as though the dog has something stuck in its throat. Sometimes there may be a nasal discharge, but generally the dog remains bright and active. Often the dog coughs when it becomes excited.

Kennel Cough is contracted when dogs are kept in close proximity, breathing in the same air and, therefore, the virus. The micro-organisms invade the respiratory system and colonise. Being viral, like the common cold, there is no treatment but vets often treat with antibiotics to prevent secondary bacterial infection. If the cough is particularly troublesome, you can give an expectorant cough medicine to help loosen the mucus.

The incubation period can be as short as three days, but more commonly it is five to seven days. The cough can be persistent and last two to three weeks, but many dogs get over it within a few days. After the dog stops coughing it can carry the infection and pass it on to others for up to 12 weeks.

There are vaccines available against some of the strains, such as Bordertella Bronchiseptica. This is is boosted every six months, and given intra-nasaly. Parainfluenza can be included in the annual booster.

Because of its name, owners often have the misconception that Kennel Cough is only contracted in a kennels environment but, in fact, dogs are at risk

The picture of health, Manorguard Adam, Crufts winner.

whenever they come together and breathe the same air in an enclosed area. The bacteria particularly like damp humid conditions and multiply rapidly in these circumstances.

Rabies

The rabies virus can infect any warm-blooded animal, including humans. The disease enters the body through a break in the skin or through the mucous membranes. It is most often passed from the saliva into a wound following a bite from an infected animal. It affects the nervous system and causes behaviour changes, but symptoms are variable and this makes initial diagnosis difficult. Some of the common behaviours displayed are: over-protectiveness, shyness, apprehensiveness, insecurity, restlessness, biting at moving or imaginary objects. There is a change in the animal's voice as the vocal chords become partially paralysed. Sometimes convulsions cause death. The animal cannot ingest food or water and so becomes dehydrated; its mouth hangs open and saliva drips from it. Eventually the animal becomes totally paralysed and dies.

Rabies is not common in every country, and authorities of some rabies-free countries operate a quarantine system for animals who are to be moved from country to country. Others operate a health passport policy. There are effective anti-rabies vaccines available and these should be administered by your vet if you live in a country where rabies is a problem, or if you intend the animal to move to an affected country.

10 Breeding Leonbergers

Before you think about breeding, you should consider the merits of neutering. If your dog or bitch is not of a high standard, you should not breed from them. It is now considered acceptable to have your dog or bitch neutered. For a male this means the surgical removal of his testicles, for a female the removal of the ovaries and uterus under a general anaesthetic. It is increasingly popular to neuter at an early age to prevent unwanted puppies for the bitch and behavioural problems in the dog.

Thirteen pups bred by Helen Matthews. Photograph by –Morgan

If you have no intention of breeding, then it makes sense to give the operation serious consideration. For the bitch, apart from unwanted puppies, it prevents the regular seasons of oestrus, and consequently unwanted attention of males, and can also help to prevent medical problems in later life. Entire females who are allowed to have seasons are more prone to conditions such as pyometra (womb infection) and mammary cancer.

Most veterinary surgeons want to spay the bitch around eight weeks after a season, but it is not a good idea to carry out the operation while the bitch is pregnant or having a false pregnancy. To give the bitch the best benefits, the operation should be carried out while she is relatively young, so speak to your vet to help you to find the optimum time.

There are even more benefits for the male because castration can have a marked effect on behaviours that can be troublesome to the ordinary pet owner or the trainer who wants to work with the dog. Castration, particularly early castration, can help to prevent, control or even eradicate some problem behaviours. If castration is being considered because of behavioural problems, it is almost certain that you will need to follow a programme of behavioural modification (training) to help the dog adjust. Although its behaviour may have been exaggerated by the amount of testosterone in its body, this also falls into the category of learnt behaviour, and so the dog needs to be 'reconditioned'! An uncastrated dog is more prone to conditions such as enlargement of the prostate gland and testicular tumours.

The optimum age at which the young male is castrated is just after he learns to cock his leg, that is, at the onset of puberty. This is when the Guide Dogs for the Blind Association castrate their young males.

People often worry about castrating a dog when they do not think twice about spaying a female. Often it is men who find it most difficult to accept. The dog does not think in the same way that we do, and leaving a dog 'intact' causes it far more mental and even physical trauma than the reduced drive that castration allows. There is no benefit in allowing him 'just one bitch', as this will not calm him down and may have just the opposite effect! Unless you intend to campaign your dog in the show ring or do something very special, it is unlikely that you will have the opportunity to use him at stud.

Dogs who have not been castrated are more likely to fight with other male dogs, more likely to elicit aggressive behaviour from other dogs, and more likely to urinate in the house, especially if another dog has been there. They tend to be more dominant and aggressive over possessions, and more likely to roam, especially if they smell a bitch on heat.

In the wild, wolves come 'on heat' only once in the early part of the year. Domestic dogs have two seasons and these can be at any time, so the male entire dog is frustrated and may be off his food many times a year. Together with the desire to become a father, this could trigger many of the behaviours that are undesirable in a domestic situation.

On the down side of castration, occasionally the coat can be affected, changing the texture. There is also the possibility that your castrated male smells a little like a bitch to other dogs, and this confusion is heightened if there is an on-heat bitch in the vicinity. But this causes far fewer problems than it would if both dogs were entire males. Also, if early castration is carried out, that is, before the dog has finished growing, he may never mature to his full potential.

Most dogs do not need as much food after they have had the surgery, because they are no longer burning up calories chasing females (mentally and physically). The appetite may improve because the reduced testosterone means that the dog is less anxious to find his mate, and food is his next most important motivator! Owners are tempted into feeding more, because the dog now has a good appetite. Therefore it is the food increase that causes weight gain, not castration.

For bitches the same applies; reduced activity of a sexual nature lessens the need for nutrition, and therefore owners must monitor weight gain and food intake and feed to maintain good condition.

Responsibilities of the Breeder

The canine breeder has many responsibilities. It is in the interests of the breed that much thought and care is taken before embarking on the breeding of Leonbergers. Understanding the faults, as well as the good points, that lie behind your foundation of breeding dogs is essential. If you are to avoid problems, it is crucial that your foundation stock is of good quality, and that you give due consideration to any faults when assessing the choice of mates.

In the interests of furthering the breed, occasionally it may be necessary to experiment with certain bloodlines but, as the breeder, you must be prepared to deal with any resulting problems in the most appropriate way. You may have sold the pups before problems become evident, so you will have to decide how to deal with both the dog and its new owners if and when this situation arises. Sometimes problems occur even when the outcome was expected to be favourable, and again these situations need to be dealt with.

Sometimes you may have to take a dog back from its owners because of changed circumstances or because they are unhappy with the animal for some reason. You are not legally compelled to do this – but most responsible breeders do so in the interests of the dog's welfare.

It is impossible for you to be sure how the pup will turn out but you should point out possible hereditary problems, and tell the potential purchaser what you have screened for and the results of these tests. You should explain what criteria you have followed, the precautions you have taken in selecting the match between parents for this particular litter, and what you have tried to achieve by so doing. This will help the purchaser assess the potential of the puppy for their own needs, and help any future breeding plans that they may have.

As a good breeder you will spend time studying, socialising and playing with the pups, building and assessing their characters. Where possible, you should have independent character assessments carried out, to help you to choose the most suitable home for each pup and to guide the prospective new owner into suitable training and social development plans. This study will help you to recognise particular traits in your bloodlines and give you a good indication and/or starting point for your future breeding plans.

You must supply purchasers with all relevant details about the individual pup, about the breed, information on how to join the breed club(s) and how to get involved in Leonberger events. You should also supply a comprehensive diet guide and information on any inoculations, veterinary treatment and worming that has already been carried out, and when the next is due.

It is also the breeder's responsibility to see that the prospective purchaser is fully conversant with the need for social and control training, both in the early weeks and months and as a continuous procedure through into maturity and beyond. Many breeders neglect this important aspect of their pup's well-being, perhaps assuming that the purchaser is already aware, or that others will give suitable advice as and when necessary. Breeders who do not educate themselves and pass on vital information of this sort may well find that behavioural problems, the result of adverse experience and learnt behaviour which could have been avoided, are more likely to be attributed to poor breeding as desperate owners search for answers.

Other added extras offered by some breeders include tattooing, books, leads, collars and other equipment. In my view you should advise prospective owners to buy and read books on training, behaviour and general care, and they should be encouraged to learn as much as they can about the breed, before they get their puppy.

Insurance

It is in your interest to sell the puppy with insurance to cover the first few weeks, and advise the purchaser to carry on this insurance for his (and your) peace of mind.

For the first few weeks after the pup goes to its new home, it is very vulnerable and its defences will not be as strong because of the stress of the change in environment. Minor ailments can develop and rapidly become major problems, and it is good to know that most problems are covered by insurance. Insurance companies vary in their offers and it is worth shopping around for the best to suit you.

Breeders' Contracts

Purchase Contracts

It is an indication that you are a good and caring breeder if you issue a contract or purchase agreement before you sell your puppies. The gist of the contract should be that the purchaser agrees to care for the welfare of the puppy for the whole of its life and if, for any reason, he needs or wishes to part with the puppy, even when it is fully grown, then you will be given first refusal as the named breeder. You could include other clauses: for example, that the purchaser attends training classes or shows the dog, but these clauses are difficult to enforce. It is worth including any exclusions that you have made on your Kennel Club registrations, thus eliminating any confusion.

The contract is really drawn up for the good of the dog and, as long as the dog is enjoying a good lifestyle and is not suffering (or, for that matter, causing) any problems due to the purchaser's negligence, then you can be content.

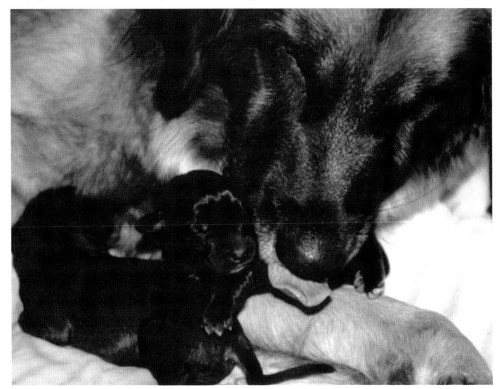

Breeders are responsible even after the puppies have left, as well as at the baby stage.

Breeding Terms

If you wish, you can sell a bitch on breeding terms. This means that the purchaser abides by a contract of breeding. Usually the purchaser pays a reduced fee for the pup (occasionally the pup is given at no charge) and then, when the bitch is bred, you take one or two puppies from the first, and sometimes subsequent litters, depending on what has been agreed.

The danger of this sort of arrangement is that often something is missed in the contract. An example is, what would happen if the bitch was deemed unsuitable to breed from and, indeed, what would make this an issue? Perhaps you would like to stipulate a certain hip score to be achieved, or that the bitch should be free from eye, elbow or other defects, and not be of a nervous or aggressive disposition. Once these are covered, there is the question of expenses – who pays for what? Will you pay for health screening charges, stud fees and travelling to stud dogs? This can be quite an expense if you add up all the costs. Also there is the issue of choosing a stud. You may find that during the time your puppy's owners have been looking after your investment, they have learned a fair amount about the breed and developed ideas different from yours of what is the ideal stud for the bitch – who will make the choice? Then when the pups are born, what if there are just a few or only one? Can you honestly expect the owners to part with the only pup if they had set their heart on keeping one?

On the plus side, if all goes to plan, both sides are happy. If the bitch is fit and the contract is sound, breeding terms can be good for both sides. The purchaser gets at reduced cost a good puppy and guidance in breeding, and you get a chance to continue your bloodline without the added burden of another bitch in the household.

Registration in the United Kingdom

The Breeder's Affix

It is a good idea to have your own affix. This is the name which, once registered with The Kennel Club, can be included in front of the registered name of any puppies that you breed, and added to the end of the registered name of any dogs that you buy in. The purpose is to give your dogs a unique identity that links them to you, and the advantages are that any one researching the breed with a view to purchasing, breeding or just for general interest knows which dogs to connect with you and whether you bred them.

Choosing an affix is fun, but not all that easy, as already more than 50,000 affixes are registered and yours must be different. Many people use made-up words, or words that mean something to them. For instance, Rikandan is made up of three names: Richard (shortened to Rik), Andrew and Daniel – the three children of Belinda and Trevor Pattrick who breed Rikandan Leonbergers. My own affix, Akamai, is the Hawaiian word for 'smart' which I discovered whilst reading a book on dolphin training in Hawaii. ('Smart' would not have been acceptable for an affix as it is a common word.)

The Kennel Club requires you to think up six possible affixes. From these they select three possibilities and these are published in The Kennel Club's monthly magazine *Kennel Gazette*, and objections invited. Once this is all over, they send you a certificate indicating your successful affix choice.

Registering the Puppies in the United Kingdom

As the breeder, you must register the litter because the new owners are not allowed to do so under The Kennel Club rules. (The exception is the Obedience and Working Trials register, but dogs on this register cannot be shown in the breed ring.) You need The Kennel Club form for application for litter registration. This

The owner is building up a trusting relationship with her Leonberger puppy.

needs to be signed by the stud dog owner to verify that their dog is the father of the puppies, and this is the same form on which you enter the names of your new puppies and send for approval to The Kennel Club.

It is easier to name the litter if you have a KC-registered affix because you can use a name that is already registered. For instance, 'Akamai Jack' would probably be accepted because, although there are many 'Jacks', there will be only one 'Akamai Jack'. On the other hand, Akamai Rossnick would be rejected because Rossnick is the registered affix of Celia Peters, another Leonberger breeder. Even the affix names of breeders of dogs other than Leonbergers would be rejected to avoid confusion.

It is best to register the litter soon after the pups are born, as the paperwork takes a while to process and, if you leave it too late, you may find the pups are ready for their new homes and the paperwork has not caught up with them.

The registration documents come through in your name as the breeder, and you need to sign and enter the relevant details on the back of the registration document in order to pass on this registration to the purchaser.

Registration Endorsements

If you wish, you can have the registration endorsed by The Kennel Club in several ways. For instance, you could add the endorsement, 'Progeny not eligible for registration'. This means that unless you see fit to lift this ban, any pups this dog produces cannot be registered. It should deter people breeding from their Leonberger for profit, as no-one will buy a pedigree dog without a registration document. Perhaps you think that the prospective buyers are not knowledgeable enough to enter into breeding. Perhaps you wish to safeguard your own selling power, that is, if other people like the pup they will have to come to you rather than ask for a pup from the sold pup. Perhaps you wish to control this particular bloodline mix for some reason, or perhaps you have recognised a fault in this pup which indicates that future breeding would be unwise.

The pup could also be registered with the endorsement, 'Not eligible for entry at shows, field trials, and working trials help under Kennel Club rules'. Normally you would apply this endorsement only if the pup has some fault which renders it outside the breed standard, and therefore you would not want the pup shown in the show ring. It would be then sold as pet quality only.

'Not eligible for issue of an export licence' prevents the purchaser from selling the pup as a registered breed abroad. However, it has been known for more unscrupulous purchasers to find ways around this.

The final endorsement is 'Name unchangeable'. The only change to the name normally allowed is the addition of an affix should the purchaser have one. This endorsement prevents that happening.

Bloodlines and Genetics

The science of dog breeding is a complex subject and there are many very good books devoted entirely to this subject. It is in your interest to read as many as possible to get a good overview of the subject and to gain a more detailed knowledge of this important area. Also it is worth obtaining copies of the Leonberger stud books for your own country and others if possible, as these give vital information on the background of numerous Leonbergers, both popular and not so well known. A stud book does not just list dogs available at stud, but is a collection of data on both sexes and often includes lists of matings and resulting litters, hip scores and other health screening information and statistics.

Line Breeding (Inbreeding)

This is one of the policies most commonly used in dog breeding. It involves mating related animals, sometimes as close as brother/sister, parent/offspring, sometimes more moderate such as cousin/cousin. The term 'inbreeding' is given to the closer matings and line breeding to the milder, less closely-related matches. The aim is to produce dogs that look alike and go on to produce puppies like themselves. It also gives the opportunity of choosing a top-class partner for your dog so that the quality of your stock is likely to improve.

Of course there are problems that can occur; whilst trying to reproduce the good points, you may also enhance the bad. The other problem is what is often termed 'inbreeding depression'. This happens if close inbreeding is carried on for several generations, and results in smaller, less healthy, pups.

Like Breeding

Breeding like to like is a commonly-used strategy, particularly by people new to breeding because line breeding sometimes goes against the moral grain.

The hope is that if you breed the best to the best, you will produce the very best. Oh, if only it was that simple! It can be very useful, and in areas such as the United Kingdom where the gene pool for Leonbergers is very limited, breeders use this strategy to try to avoid doubling up on weakness. But this style of mating is very hit and miss, and you are never quite sure what the outcome will be. You may find that you bring to the forefront a hitherto unnoticed fault or strength in those individuals.

Unlike Matings

This is where breeders use a mate totally unlike their own dog to try to compensate for a fault, for example, mating a dog who is too long in the back to a bitch who is too short, in the hope that the pups will come out 'about right'. This sometimes works as a short-term measure, although often you will produce some of each. Any pups who do come out 'about right' tend to go on to produce pups with the original faults.

Breeding the Perfect Leonberger

Perhaps this heading *is* a little ambitious. If it were this simple we would produce perfect animals from every mating. We should first look at everything from the dog's point of view. As breeders of Leonbergers, we are not developing physical abnormalities causing distress, laboured breathing or spinal problems, for the sake of reaching an 'ideal'. We have, however, developed a few abnormalities that the dog would do better without, such as hip dysplasia (HD), osteochondritis dissecans (OCD), Entropia, Ectropia and perhaps a few other minor imperfections (from the point of view of impact on the dog), such as umbilical hernia, wrong tail carriage and incorrect colour. There are some problems for which certain lines may show more of a tendency than others, such as torsion, colitis, cancer, Addison's disease, sensitivity to anaesthesia, heart problems. There are yet other areas that give cause for possible concern; for instance, at present we are screening for the possibility of hereditary cataracts.

By looking at the bloodlines and pedigrees of several generations, it can be determined whether or not the majority of defects is likely to have a genetic basis. However, you should bear in mind that all these defects can be a result of external influence and nothing to do with genetics. Until we know for certain that the defect was caused by circumstances that were not genetic, then we should avoid using the affected dog in the breeding programme, unless the problem is trivial and the dog otherwise outstanding. In using a dog with even a minor defect you should be aware that at least some of the puppies will have the same defect and the others will be carriers.

The difficulty arises when your dog is a *carrier* of a certain defect, because it seems normal. Unless you are very knowledgeable about its ancestry, not to mention the rest of the litter, you may never know that your dog is a carrier until you breed from it, perhaps to another carrier.

Threshold Traits

A number of abnormalities are due to the complex effect of several genes, all of which affect a certain characteristic. When pooled together, the genes manifest themselves in the most extreme form whilst, if coming together in fewer numbers, their effect is unnoticeable. Cryptorchidism is thought to be a result of this, and can come in degrees of severity, from a lateness of one of the testes to drop into the scrotum, to a refusal to drop into the correct position at all.

Mutations

From time to time, nature throws in a mutation, which is how all the different species evolved initially. Over the years breeders have made use of these mutations, taking them as a basis for a breed. Breeders are not as stringent as nature and that is why abnormalities detrimental to the dog have been allowed to develop. In nature, abnormalities only survive if they are an advantage to the animal.

Genes can also be influenced and changed by external factors, such as X-rays and other exposure to radiation and chemical pollutants.

A good male exudes masculinity.

Chapter 10

The Stud Dog

The decision to use a certain dog at stud should be multi-factored. First, your chosen sire must be a good specimen of the breed. If you are a novice, a good starting point is to look at dogs that have won consistently in the show ring under many different judges. If you want to breed for a working Leonberger, choose a stud with a good track record, showing the correct stable yet outgoing and lively temperament. A dog that wins in the show ring or displays good conformation often makes a good working dog should the owner wish to take it in that direction. Good physical structure is an important part of a working dog's attributes. As yet, we have not produced types of Leos more suited to work and less suited to the show ring as in some breeds, but you will find some lines, as well as individuals within litters, where the dogs have a better temperament for working than others.

Probably the most important factor in choosing your stud is temperament and stability of character, but upbringing and environment have much influence on this.

A good male Leonberger, whatever his background, should exude masculinity, quality and presence.

Once you develop an 'eye' for a good dog, you will be able to identify good and bad points in animals that have not been shown, and may decide that it is better to use a lesser-known and, therefore, usually lesser-used stud dog. You need to look at many dogs and evaluate their movement, overall look and temperament in order to do this.

This is just the start. Once you have identified a dog (or several dogs) that you like, you must then look carefully at his pedigree and compare it to your bitch's. Then you must look at other relations of this dog to research the good and bad points that have evolved from this line. If possible, look at progeny already born from him, and talk to the owners of these dogs. Talk to as many other breeders and people who have been in the breed a long time as you can.

Naturally, you should talk to the owners of the stud dog to see how they feel about the match: if they are willing to allow their dog to be used on your bitch, what their conditions of mating are, and how 'busy' the dog is likely to be at the appropriate time. Also, ask for copies of all health screening checks: a copy of the hip score, eye test, and any other documents. If you have any doubts, these can be verified by the appropriate bodies.

If the dog has not been used at stud before, make sure that the owner is fully aware of the various tests that are required and that they must be done before you make your final decision.

In some countries it is necessary for the dog to be licensed for breeding. This licence is granted depending on the dog's characteristics, temperament, physical appearance, structure and inherited characteristics. The licence is not granted if the dog does not meet the standard set down for the breed.

Care and Duties of the Stud Dog

Care of the stud dog, or potential stud dog, starts when he is very young. He needs to be educated in canine ways. A dog that is brought up alone, separated from his siblings too soon or denied the opportunity to interact with other dogs, both male and female, will not be easy to adapt to stud work. He needs to play (some of the play has sexual connotations), and find his position in the hierarchy, both within the family unit and with other dogs, so that his character develops and he becomes self assured without feeling the need to resort to aggression. He needs to accept your handling readily, as you may need to assist at some point in the mating procedure, if only to stop the dogs walking around once tied, and you do not want him to feel uncomfortable or threatened by your presence.

The stud dog, if he becomes popular, may have to 'work' quite hard, particularly in the spring when more bitches come into season. He must be kept in good, hard condition. He should be given a good-quality, balanced diet, adjusted according to his work-load, both from his stud work and the rest of his routine. It is unlikely that any supplements are necessary if his diet is of premium quality.

If at all possible, his first bitch should be quiet and experienced and therefore less likely to be awkward or aggressive. It is common practice for stud dog owners to use one of their own house bitches to prove a stud where possible and then, when a litter is born and all the puppies are normal and healthy, offer the dog's services to outside bitches. If this is not possible, often a first mating takes place with the stud fee waived, deferred or a pup back in lieu, to prove the dog.

On a first mating it is important to encourage the dog as much as possible. If it can arranged, let him run free with the bitch for a few days, allowing him to practise the art without any pressure from anxious owners. It also will help him if his partner is a very forward bitch he already knows, who will encourage rather than deter him on his first experience.

The brood bitch should be healthy and fit.

It is important to maintain a routine for the stud, and it is usual for the dog to work at home, that is, the bitches are brought to him. Try to mate him in the same place, using the same routine each time, and he will learn what to expect. This will enhance his sexual arousal and so aid matings, particularly if a bitch plays 'hard to get'.

The stud dog owner has to accept that not all bitches will be presented for mating at the correct time. This can be frustrating for all concerned, and certainly the inexperienced stud may lose interest if this occurs too often. Some Leonberger bitches stay receptive only for a very short time and it makes sense for bitch owners to be too early rather than too late. This is where the owners of studs with spare accommodation, at least for the dogs, will win. Being able to allow the bitch to stay on site or nearby until the time is right helps enormously. Some stud owners even allow the bitches to be kennelled with the dog until a satisfactory mating occurs. The gentler males settle down and enjoy this luxury, and the females relax after a little while if they are well socialised and accustomed to being with other dogs.

Stud dog owners need to be very patient with bitch owners and, where a mating is not achieved, give an invitation to come back. On the other hand, the stud owner cannot be expected to make his dog available solely to one bitch, and other bookings may need to be taken into consideration and given priority.

The stud owner should make sure that the bitch owner is fully aware of all conditions and arrangements. This includes the fee, which in Leonbergers normally is the same as the standard price of a puppy. The price of a top-winning dog or an imported dog is likely to be a little higher than that of a less well-known or less sought-after dog.

What are the possible problems of breeding? Perhaps the bitch will not get pregnant. Most stud owners offer a repeat mating next time around. Some Leonberger stud owners offer a repeat mating if the litter is small (say, four or less puppies). In some countries, it is customary to have a split payment system where the bitch owner pays half of the stud fee at mating and the other half when the puppies are born safely. Whatever you decide, it is best to put it in writing to form a contract between you and the owner of the bitch so that you both know where you stand.

In some parts of the world it is required that all breeding stock is permanently identified by tattoo. As the breed becomes numerically larger it may become difficult to be sure that the dog you are mating is the correct one according to the papers without some form of permanent identification.

It is well worth while having your dog's semen regularly checked by a veterinary surgeon, and certainly tested following any infertile matings or illness. The semen that the stud dog uses will have been made several months previously, so keep a diary of any illness, raised temperature or even extremes in weather conditions that might affect the quality of his semen.

Artificial Insemination (AI)

In countries such as the United Kingdom where quarantine is still in force, artificial insemination can be a favourable alternative to subjecting a dog to the trauma of six months in a quarantine kennel. All paperwork must be correct, and the AI should be carried out by an experienced veterinary surgeon.

The official route for using imported semen is rather long and complicated, but if you do not follow it the resulting puppies cannot be registered. If you want to take this path, then first you need to identify a suitable dog, free from hereditary defects, that will greatly benefit the stock in this country.

The Kennel Club has to be given evidence that there is good reason for the semen to be imported and used, and also evidence that the bitch it is to be used on is of good quality and does not have genetic defects. The Kennel Club then puts the idea before a committee and subcommittee before making its decision which may not be favourable. The breeder can appeal against the decision and bring forward more evidence.

The Ministry of Agriculture, Fisheries and Food (MAFF) controls the import of canine semen into the United Kingdom. Once a favourable decision has been made by The Kennel Club, MAFF has to be approached to import the semen. This procedure can take up to four weeks. The application will be granted on the same lines as bringing a dog into the country, that is, the donor dog must have been kept in a rabies-free area, and must not have come into contact with rabies for at least six months, or the semen must stay in quarantine for six months in this country, and the donor dog monitored for the same period in his own country.

The semen is stored in glass ampoules called straws, which are frozen and kept in liquid nitrogen at a collection agency, usually a veterinary school. When the bitch comes into season she is taken to the semen and, after tests to see when she ovulates, she is inseminated.

All this attracts considerable costs, with payments due to the stud dog owner, vets, MAFF, The Kennel Club, the storage facility and transportation of what is classed as a dangerous cargo. At the end of the day it can cost about the same as the import of a stud dog.

The Brood Bitch

A brood bitch must be a good specimen of the breed, but it is also important that she is not nervous, as this can be passed on to her young as a learned behaviour before they leave her nest. To ensure the best chance of a successful and problem-free mating, pregnancy, and birth she must be fit, displaying a well-muscled, hard condition, full of vigour, and neither under- nor overweight.

Well before her season and planned mating, she should be checked for hereditary faults (see Chapter 9), and your Leonberger club can update you on current areas for concern and acceptable or desirable scores. If you do not have the tests done, stud dog owners will not allow you to use their animals. If you find that the results are unsatisfactory, you should refrain from breeding from your bitch.

Worming and inoculations (or blood tests for immunity levels) should be checked and, where necessary, updated to make sure that the pups have a good start.

The potential brood bitch needs no special diet, but a good-quality, well-balanced diet is essential for all Leonbergers.

Chapter 10

Just as with the stud dog, care must be taken in the early weeks and months of the bitch's life to allow her to learn how to mix and socialise with other dogs. Some matings are a trauma for the bitch, and this is particularly the case if she is not accustomed to being with, or socialising with, other dogs. If she is used to living in a home environment with only humans for company, the attention of a large male with only one thing on his mind can be an ordeal even if, in theory, she is ready to mate.

Occasionally your bitch may show a preference to mate only with a specific male who may not be your choice. This is not your bitch being awkward; it is a very natural part of behaviour, which goes back to the dog's wolf origins. Whenever possible, wolves pair for life. You can normally get around this by allowing the bitch to become better acquainted with your chosen suitor in the absence of the other male.

Seasons (Oestrus)

Some Leonbergers have erratic seasons or more than the accepted norm(about every six months). Regularity and 'normality' of the seasons can be affected by many things, such as trauma, change of environment, change of owner, ill health, weather and even other bitches coming into season in the immediate vicinity. Where a number of bitches live together, after a while they may 'cycle' together. Cold weather can delay seasons, whilst a warm spell in the spring tends to bring bitches into season en masse. However, once you have grown used to your bitch and witnessed a few of her seasons, you should be able to predict the onset of oestrus with a fair degree of accuracy.

While the bitch is not 'in season', she is said to be 'anoestrus'. Pro-oestrus is the beginning of the season when oestrogen levels rise and the bitch may behave differently; some bitches become more subdued, others become restless. She may pay more attention to her genital region, with more frequent washing. During exercise she is more likely to urinate in many spots, presumably to advertise her condition to prospective suitors. Certainly, males become more aware of her presence than normal, and you must take care to protect her from unwanted dogs; otherwise you could find your Leonberger giving birth to crossbreed pups which, whilst they may be cute, do not have the same appeal to the discerning Leonberger fancier! It is not uncommon for other females to be attracted to your bitch in pro-oestrus. She may even go through the motions of mating with either sex, although in pro-oestrus she is not fertile.

The vulva swells, and becomes progressively more swollen as the oestrus approaches. There is a discharge from the vulva: the quantity and type varies from bitch to bitch and from season to season. Normally the discharge is blood-suffused. Occasionally a bitch may have a 'silent' season, which means that although there is swelling, there is little or no bloody discharge.

The average time for the onset of oestrus is about nine to ten days after the start of pro-oestrus, but it is not uncommon in Leonbergers for a bitch to enter oestrus much earlier. Or perhaps pro-oestrus has not been recognised because the signs are too slight, and suddenly the bitch is ready to mate.

The average length of time the bitch stays fertile and ready to mate is about seven days, but in reality it is seldom this long. Some breeders have reported bitches being 'ready' for less than a few hours, whilst others have had bitches that have readily accepted males up to three weeks after the onset of oestrus.

With the onset of oestrus the swollen vulva becomes flabby and may be hot to the touch, hence the term 'on heat'. The discharge may turn clear or a yellow colour, and the bitch signals her readiness with a willingness to 'stand'. She may put on a display of readiness by lifting her tail up and over her back, elevating and displaying the vulva in a very characteristic manner. This behaviour may be brought on by the presence of other animals in the household, or you should be able to stimulate it by applying gentle pressure on her back at the base of her tail.

Some vets can give a blood or cytology test to tell you what stage the bitch is at in her cycle. This can be costly if you want to know the exact position, as tests may be necessary over a period of days to discover the point at which the bitch is going over into oestrus. Many breeders find the tests well worth the investment, as catching the bitch at the optimum time can increase litter size. It is ideal to prove that the dog has not yet ovulated, particularly if you have a long way to travel, as you can plan accordingly.

Once your Leo bitch has ovulated she should be mated within a few hours in case this is all the time that there will be. If you delay the mating by trying to fit it in with your lifestyle, you may find that your time is wasted. The bitch may be put under unnecessary stress from the male and, perhaps, the interference of anxious breeders when really her time has passed. Unfortunately, the biological process does not wait to fit around a work or domestic schedule.

Refusal to mate can be caused by medical reasons such as growths, obstructions, vaginal polyps or other abnormalities and, in these cases, veterinary assistance must be sought. It is more often the case that the bitch simply is not ready; it is either too late or too early in her season, and nature does not allow her to accept the male.

Bitches should not be bred from until they are mature physically, which is about two years for a Leo. The upper age limit should be no more than seven or eight years, as by this time the Leonberger is in old age, having an average lifespan of around 10 years. Because the Leonberger as a breed tends to produce large litters, it is best to allow a good period of rehabilitation between litters. In many breeds, it is acceptable to miss one season and breed on the next but if your Leo, like so many, has seasons more frequently than every six months, leave at least a year between litters and then go ahead only if the bitch is fit and fully recovered.

The Leonberger breed clubs have a code of practice and guidelines for breeders to help safeguard the best interests of the breed. The information given by the breed clubs is constantly updated by enthusiastic members. If you breed, you should inform the club of your litter details so that the records can be updated.

Mating Leonbergers

Having done all your homework in selecting your bitch's mate, getting the time right and so on, hopefully, now is the 'right time' to proceed with the mating.

It is customary and best for the bitch to go to the dog on his territory. On arrival, allow the bitch the opportunity to urinate and defecate, take a small drink and generally make herself comfortable and adjust to her surroundings before she meets her suitor. As with any other 'exercise', it is best not to feed or allow excessive drinking immediately before or after the act.

The stud dog owner may want to check identity and paperwork before proceeding, so leave your bitch in the car until you are shown where the mating will take place, and have discussed and accustomed yourself to the stud dog owner's wishes. Some will suggest that the dogs run free together in a controlled environment, the thrill of the chase increasing the dog's libido. Others prefer that the two are kept on lead and collar, and certainly this is a good idea, at least until the reactions of the potential partners can be assessed. Once you are sure that the two will be friendly, they can be allowed some freedom in a safe fenced area to flirt and play.

The dog will sniff and lick the bitch's vulva.

The dog will sniff and lick the bitch's vulva and perhaps her hind legs which helps stimulate her, but this may be unnecessary in the case of a bitch that is ready. If the bitch is ready she indicates this by raising her tail and standing braced to take the dog's weight. Her vulva is exposed and raised. The dog may test her by placing his head on her back, and perhaps lick her briefly before mounting, usually from the rear. At this stage the dog may not penetrate correctly or the bitch may dislodge him by turning or jumping around and they will resort to foreplay. The procedure starts again, but if the bitch continues to jump around, it is best to hold her to allow the dog to penetrate.

The dog clasps the bitch with his fore legs.

The dog clasps the bitch with his fore legs and thrusts his penis towards the vulva. Experienced stud dogs can be very accurate and achieve penetration after only a few thrusts. If there is a big difference in height between the dog and bitch he may need a little guidance, or the height of one of the animals changed by standing it on a step or even a book. Sometimes it is useful to guide the dog's penis in by hand, but this presents obvious risks from an infection point of view and the dog may not take kindly to being touched in this area, particularly if he is not used to it.

If you are not already holding the dogs, now move in calmly to control the situation. The reasons the dogs need to be held at this point are varied. The Leonberger male will undoubtedly be larger and heavier than the bitch, and she

The tie.

will appreciate some assistance with his weight; a well-positioned knee under the abdomen is very helpful. Also it is not unusual for the animals to start walking around and this could put unnecessary stress on the genitalia of both partners. At the beginning of the penetration it may be painful or at least uncomfortable for the bitch and she may try to break free. Firm, kind control is called for from the owners.

It is not uncommon for a bitch to be very vocal. Maiden bitches may try hard to pull away and make a lot of noise, particularly as the penetration becomes more intense. Once penetration has been fully accomplished the resistance changes to a more resigned groan and many bitches pant and drool throughout the procedure.

After a few moments (sometimes a few minutes), the dog tries to lift one leg over the bitch's back to allow him to turn into the 'tie position' (see photograph page 105). Stud owners often help here to give a smooth turn. This really is a two-person job, one for each dog. In my experience, a third person is invaluable to bring chairs to slip under aching human bodies as a tie may last an average of 15–20 minutes, but could be almost an hour! Do not be unduly worried, however, if the tie lasts just a few minutes, as a bitch can conceive even without a tie. Psychologically, breeders are happier with a 'good tie'.

If you are not happy because your bitch is resisting, or you are inclined to excite the bitch, then perhaps you could take on the chair positioning and coffee-making jobs, whilst more experienced breeders get on with controlling the dogs.

The dogs often become bored and some even fall asleep during the tie, particularly if it is prolonged, and you must be vigilant to prevent any problems.

When they are ready the dogs break free, and should be returned to their own familiar places to rest and have a drink.

It is usual to mate the dog again, perhaps the next day, but this is not necessary if the mating was successful; it is more a case of breeders making sure.

If the bitch is taken and left with the stud it is customary for a photograph to be taken of the tie to serve as proof that the mating took place, and to the correct dog.

Following the successful mating all that is left to do is pay the stud fee, and complete the paperwork. The bitch owner needs a signed document from the stud owner to prove to The Kennel Club that the mating took place.

The Pregnancy

Once mating has taken place successfully, it is normal to assume that the bitch is pregnant until proved otherwise. Keep her away from all other male dogs until you are sure her season has finished. Sometimes the mating seems to make the end of the season sooner, but it can go on a further one or even two weeks.

The bitch needs no special diet or treatment at this point, but try to keep her away from areas where there is a high risk of infection or disease, and definitely away from any ill dogs. You should also avoid causing her any stress, so return to her normal routine. The first three weeks are very important as it is not until this point that the placenta attaches to the uterine wall, so there is a higher risk of abortion at this early stage.

At around the fourth week, vets and experienced breeders can palpate the bitch's abdomen gently and determine if she is indeed pregnant as they can feel the developing puppies surrounded by a bag of embryonic fluid, like little balls. To feel these the bitch needs to be relaxed, and it is more difficult if she is overweight. Palpation should be carried out only by an experienced person or a vet as it does carry some risk of damaging the embryos.

Ultrasound scanning can also be carried out around this time, in much the same way as for humans, although diagnosis does depend on the skill of the operator. I have found scanning to be very accurate and a useful guide of how many puppies to expect, always a good thing to know when whelping, and also helpful when pre-booking the pups' new homes. Ultrasound can be used to diagnose the early signs of pyometra, a

At 30 days in whelp the embryos can be clearly seen on the ultrasound scan.

Ultrasound scanning by a competent scanner such as Dominee can save a lot of worry.

Some bitches have more erratic seasons than the norm.

life-threatening bacterial infection, and *hydrops foetalis*, a condition where the foetus becomes enlarged with fluid.

At about five weeks, the fluid and tissue surrounding the embryos increase and palpation becomes increasingly difficult but by this time the bitch is showing other signs.

Although the bitch may seem to be more rotund than normal, it is not necessary to increase her food intake until the sixth week of pregnancy. This should be done gradually until by the ninth week she is on about 1.5 times her normal feed. Split the food into two or three meals but her normal well-balanced diet is all that is necessary. If you increase the bulk or nutrition too much the puppies may grow abnormally.

Some Leonbergers are reluctant to eat at the best of times, but you should not worry about this unless it becomes excessive or the bitch becomes under-weight. Often the lack of appetite is linked to a more sedate lifestyle and sometimes regular exercise of a quality nature and a little mental stimulation and fresh air puts things right.

As the pregnancy goes into its last couple of weeks, give your bitch a diet specifically formulated for pregnant and lactating bitches to ensure that she is getting all the nutrition she needs. Some breeders prefer to make up their own diets from raw materials, but this is time-consuming and quite difficult and only the most dedicated get the balance right. I prefer to leave this to the experts so use a premium quality all-in-one food specifically designed for the job, and then I can concentrate my energies into looking after the dog's other needs.

Generally, Leonbergers are happy to laze around and this applies particularly when they are pregnant and the environment is calm. However, it is essential that a pregnant Leo gets regular, moderate exercise. I am not suggesting that she should charge around like a mad thing, but a good walk to keep the muscles in trim is very important so that your bitch has the best chance of an easy birth. Sometimes a bitch is extremely active and has to be persuaded to take sufficient rest by being put in a quiet area and gently restricted to ensure that she does take it easy and allows the pups to grow normally inside.

Towards the end of the pregnancy it is important that your bitch gets used to the area that has been set aside for whelping so that she can be comfortable there.

Preparation for Whelping

The first thing to consider about whelping is where it is going to take place. Some breeders have one area set aside for the pups when they are very young, perhaps in the house, and then another area as they get older and more mobile. Others have one area that is adjusted as the litter progresses; much depends on your own situation. Bear in mind that, in the interests of rearing the whole litter and preventing the bitch crushing any pups, you will be spending a lot of time with them, and most breeders like to rig up a comfortable bed or sofa so that they can hold their vigil in relative comfort. If you do not hold a 24-hour guard so that you can rescue any distressed pups from your bitch's well-meaning but heavy bulk, resign yourself to the fact that you could have one or two fatalities, if not more. Take heart: after about a week the bitch will choose to spend some time away from the whelping area, and you will be able to make the most of this by relaxing or catching up on jobs. The nights become more settled also as the pups go longer between feeds, so sleep is possible for you!

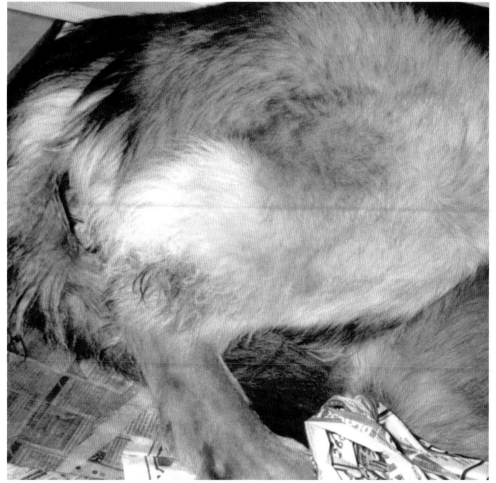

Contractions may be evident. The bitch will lift her tail or may even stand or squat.

The bitch needs a warm, enclosed area that is easily cleaned, secure and out of harm's way. She needs a whelping box large enough to allow her to lie down flat with her puppies, stand up, walk around and reposition herself. If the box is too small, she will be anxious about crushing the pups and her concern may turn to a lack of interest because she cannot get comfortable.

In common with many large, heavy breeds, Leonbergers do tend to be clumsy, and therefore a rail around the inside perimeter of the box is essential to prevent her from crushing the pups as she lies down or leans back.

Bedding should be easy to wash and dry, and the fur fabric available from most big dog shows and pet shops is ideal. Also you need a good supply of clean newspapers to line the box, absorb any moisture and,

The bitch may be a little confused at first, but most take some interest. In general, Leos are very maternal.

later, mop up all the little accidents in the area where the pups play.

The room temperature of the whelping area is important. It should be kept at around 24°C (75°F) for the first 10 days. If you need some form of extra heating, infra-red lamps or heat pads are ideal but otherwise the bitch supplies all the extra heat that is required. If you are relying on central heating, remember to keep it on at night or the temperature may drop too low for newly-born pups.

If you have never whelped a bitch before, read up as much as you can. This book is merely a guide and is not intended as a definitive work on whelping; there is much more to learn. If possible, enlist the help of an experienced breeder who may not be there at the birth but at least may be able to give you a few tips beforehand.

Whelping can be a very lonely time for the breeder, and there are times when help may be needed. It is always of great comfort to have an extra pair of hands, someone that the bitch is familiar with, if only to weigh pups, pass clean cloths and make coffee.

The pups are wet and can soon chill, so temperature control is important.

Whelping

When the bitch is nearly ready to whelp she might tremble, become agitated, vomit, search for bed areas, and shred up newspapers or anything else that she deems suitable bedding material. This phase can be quite short or can go on for 24–48 hours. As the time approaches, even an experienced bitch may be unsure of what is happening, and often thinks that she needs to relieve herself when really the first puppy is on its way.

As the contractions start to become apparent then you know that the pup is imminent, although the physical signs of contractions may be difficult to detect in some Leonbergers. Listen, as often the bitch groans as the contractions come to a climax. Most bitches have their pups without any help from their owners,

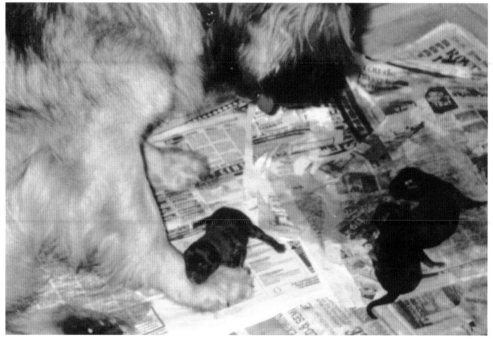

For the maiden bitch, this can take a bit of getting used to!

but sometimes the birthing procedure is difficult because of the position of the pup or other obstruction. This is when all your reading comes in useful and you find that most situations can be coped with. However, any delay in calling for expert help when it is needed may risk the survival of a pup or, indeed, your bitch, so if you have any doubt you should have no hesitation in calling the vet.

If the bitch fails to take immediate interest in the pup, intervene carefully, making sure that the foetal sac is broken open. Do it yourself if it is not, and the pup can then take its first breath of air. The bitch often takes over when she sees you working on the pup but, if not, you need to make sure that the umbilical cord has broken away from the placenta, and it may be necessary to cut it yourself. Simulate the bitch's rough-tongued wash by rubbing the pup in clean towelling until it is moving around and breathing normally, and then place it between the bitch's front paws for her to wash. Then put the pup on to a nipple to encourage it to take its first meal of the all-important colostrum-rich milk.

Some pups take in fluid during the birthing process, and this can be heard as a rattling sound in the breathing. To help get rid of this, first wrap the pup in a piece of towelling to stop it slipping and hold it down by your side, firmly supporting its head. Swing the pup in a large arc, head pointing down. After a few swings give the pup another rub and check its condition. Repeat if necessary until the airway is clear. This procedure is also worth doing if a pup comes out not breathing at all, and gentle blowing into the pup's mouth can also help to stimulate a reaction. I have revived many pups in this way and all have survived to live healthy lives. I once spent 15 minutes reviving a collie pup and I still have her 12 years later. Lack of any response after a few minutes suggests that the pup is not going to make it, and it is best to not continue. As with humans, damage occurs if the brain is starved of oxygen and you could end up reviving a brain-damaged pup.

If the bitch strains unproductively for more than a couple of hours then you definitely need to enlist the services of your vet. Anything more than a three-hour gap between puppies, even without straining, could indicate a problem.

Newborn Leonbergers

It is not easy to tell newly-born Leonberger pups apart, and one of the favourite methods of identification is to tie different-coloured ribbon around each pup's neck as it is born, and use this colour coding for future reference. The ribbons need to be changed at regular intervals, but they help to ensure that every pup receives individual attention and its progress is monitored. There are other means of identification: some breeders cut out a little fur in different places, others use animal markers, but the ribbons certainly help to give the pups individuality from an early age.

Once they are all safely delivered, the interesting, very tiring, part starts. Mortality is most common at birth and in the first week of life, but many deaths can be avoided by good and vigilant management of the bitch and her puppies. The pups are highly susceptible to disease and infection, they cannot control their own temperature and they are very easily crushed, the weight of the mother's body preventing or muffling any cries.

Once all the puppies are born and have taken their first all-important feed, mum can settle down to a well-earned rest.

By the time all the pups are safely delivered and have taken their first feed, and the bitch's needs have been attended to, you will be rather tired yourself. Once you are satisfied that all is calm, it is time to enlist the help of a friend or partner to step in and puppy watch while you take time out to freshen up and get a few hours' sleep.

Most Leonbergers have 10 teats, but it is not unusual for some of them not to be serviceable so it may be necessary to supplement the food supply, particularly if there are more than nine pups. It is best to try to give the pups their mother's milk as much as possible, so the breeder makes sure that smaller or less robust pups get the first go whenever possible, moving the pups around to make sure that they all get their fair share.

As the pups grow, particularly over the first week or so, there will be times when it is obvious that they are not satisfied by the amount of milk available, and suck at the bitch and cry pitifully. As long as this does not go on for too long you need not worry. It is not possible for the bitch to provide the perfect amount of milk all the time, and she needs to produce an ever-increasing amount for the hungry pups. Their persistence and nagging on the empty mammary glands help stimulate the milk flow, and soon you will find that the pups will be fed and settled. Therefore be very sure that your bitch does not have enough milk of her own before introducing a substitute milk.

If you have to give supplementary milk, try to ensure that all the pups get some natural milk as well. Strict hygiene must be observed in the preparation of

Daily weighing helps to ensure that all the puppies are doing well and identifies any that need special attention.

the milk to avoid infection, and you should follow the manufacturer's directions exactly when making up the bitch milk substitute.

Weigh the pups daily in the first couple of weeks to get a good indication of how they are progressing and which pups need special help. Check that the identifying ribbons are not getting too tight, and replace where necessary. Birth weight and gain depend on litter size and individual bitches. Birth weights can vary between 225g–0.45kg (8oz–1lb) but as long as the pup appears well proportioned and strong, it is best to let common sense prevail, allow nature to take its course, and not get too

Bitches are often reluctant to leave the puppies during the first few days so a meal in the whelping box will be very welcome.

Gradual weight gain is best.

mentally tied up with such concerns as correct weight for age. Having said that, pups under 283g (10oz) should be monitored carefully. Gradual weight gain and development is better physically for the pup than a rapid growth rate. Some veterinary experts link rapid growth rate to a number of bone and muscle complaints, including permanent defects such as Hip Dysplasia.

There is always much discussion surrounding feeding, and protein levels in particular. Some Leonberger breeders decry the use of high protein diets and never use more than a 24% protein level, while others successfully rear superb litters using prepared diets with protein levels of around 30%.

As the pups develop and grow, so their intake of milk from the bitch increases. Nature allows for this, but you need to increase the amount of food you give the bitch. The amount varies depending on litter size, but usually the increase is made gradually until at about three weeks after the birth she is eating three times her normal amount of food. Water intake also increases dramatically as the fluids are taken from her body. Expect the pups to double their birth weight in 7–9 days, although this can be a little sooner in smaller litters.

Try to establish a routine for day and night. It is tempting to leave the pups with a light on all the time, but this is not really good for them and there needs to be some differentiation. For the first two to three weeks a lamp with subdued lighting should be adequate for you to make sure that all the pups are safe at night. Later, when the bitch is away from the pups for periods of time the lights should be turned off and the room quiet at night to help the pups develop a natural cycle.

Development of Leo Pups

It is up to you to care for the physical and mental needs of both bitch and pups. The pups become more and more interesting as they develop, and need more

It is a good idea to keep a photographic record – the numbers help to identify who is who.

At around two weeks, eyes and ears open and the pups start to take more interest in their surroundings.

That first solid meal is rather hit and miss!

However, they get the idea within a few days.

Mum gets some help with the cuddling.

stimulation to keep them occupied and provide them with a stable character with which to start their new lives.

The pups gradually strengthen, and as early as two to three days you will see little tails wagging as their owners compete for the best teat. At seven to nine days you see them raising themselves up to get a better feeding position.

Over the first few days of life make a careful check on the pups' overall health and condition. Any abnormalities should be checked out by the vet and advice followed. Hind dew claws should be removed around the fourth or fifth day; at this time the pain receptors are not developed properly and the pup is used to being handled a little so, as long as the job is done correctly, the pup suffers no trauma. Ask the vet to call, who can check out the whole litter and the bitch at the same time.

At about two weeks the eyes and ears start to open, and the pups are more aware of their surroundings. Now treat them for worms and repeat this procedure every two weeks until they are six or eight weeks old. Worming preparations are usually best purchased from your vet.

At approximately three weeks the pups start to show signs that mother's milk is not enough, and so the weaning process begins. This is rather a messy affair. Puppy food comes in various types and many excellent foods are ready prepared, easy to use, and very palatable to young pups.

To start the weaning, offer a dish full of puppy milk or very moist puppy formula food while the bitch is absent. The pups will soon show interest and any that don't can be placed by the bowl and a little food smeared on their mouths to help them get the idea. When they have had their fill (which will be very little to start with), allow the bitch back and let her finish off the remaining food. Gradually offer food more frequently until you are giving four or five feeds a day. The amount should be as much as the pups can eat in one sitting, and any uneaten food should be taken away and discarded, or fed to the bitch. Water should be made available in a low, non-tip dish.

By about four and half to five weeks old the bitch will spend less time with the pups and, by restricting her visits, she will help you to wean them off her. You will find she is quite keen to get away from them sometimes.

The best age to let the puppies go to their new homes is around seven to eight weeks. This means each pup has had the benefit of the interaction with the rest of the litter. It has learnt to accept new situations and is still in that critical socialisation period so that you can introduce it to new situations in your home and local environment.

At around four weeks the pups are very active in a rather clumsy and endearing way.

Behaviour and Social Training

Behavioural Development

It is most important that all breeders and owners understand a pup's development, not just from the physical aspect but from the behavioural point of view.

Our domestic dog evolved from the wolf and there is still a strong element of instinctive wolf behaviour and influence which dictates how the dog reacts. The Leonberger, like any other breed, reacts in a very similar way to the young wolf in the wild in that it has the ability to adapt to the environment and relate to the objects and other animals around it, be it canine or otherwise.

Food plays a major part in shaping and dictating the dog's behaviour patterns, as does the sexual drive to reproduce. The availability of both these all-important motivators has a marked effect on the dog's behaviour and struggle for supremacy. As your Leo goes through the developmental process, it tries out, practises and develops the skills that it needs to aid its individual survival and, indeed, that of its own progeny.

The Leonberger puppy's behavioural development can be broken down into seven different phases: the prenatal period, the neonatal period, the transitional period, the socialisation period, the juvenile period, the adolescent period and adulthood. Each period of the dog's development holds separate and yet linked factors, and trauma at the wrong time can have lasting effects. At the beginning, the development periods are measured in weeks, and then later in months, but this serves merely as a guideline. Pups vary, often quite remarkably, from these parameters. Variations can be related to individual circumstances surrounding the litter, the bloodlines and the new home.

For the first two weeks the pups eat, sleep and grow!

The Prenatal Period

Research shows that an influence on eventual behaviour and development can result from factors taking place before the pup is born. Proper nutrition, fitness and warmth for the mother have a marked effect on the resulting progeny. Care during all stages will help to ensure good mental and physical health.

The puppy is extremely influenced by its environment.

The Neonatal Period

This covers the first two weeks of the pup's life. The pup is completely dependent on its mother during this time and almost all its social interaction is only with the mother. It spends its time sleeping and eating. Its brain is still maturing. Early gentle handling helps it to develop and is good for its emotional balance. It is sensitive to external temperature, touch, pain and taste, but cannot regulate its own temperature. Towards the latter part of this period the pup's eyes and ears start to open, but it is not until the next important stage that the pup responds to light, movement and loud noise.

The Transitional Period

This is the period when the pup really becomes aware of its surroundings. From two to four weeks, the pup goes from complete dependency to acquiring some skills that give it a degree of independence. It begins to walk rather than crawl, and can go backwards as well as forwards. It reacts to movement and sounds, recognises people and, towards the end of the transitional period, starts to show other behaviours such as barking, growling, tail wagging, raising of a paw and play. It develops the ability to urinate and defecate outside the nest.

The Socialisation Period

Now the fun really starts for the Leonberger pup, breeder and, if they are around, the potential owners. The period (sometimes termed the critical period due to its influence on future behaviour), covers from 4 to between 12 and 16 weeks. At the beginning of this period the pup has relatively well-developed sensory and motor skills, and it is ready for learning in a more complex way. Slowly the pup is becoming equipped to deal with its environment. There is a gradual progression in the dog's abilities and, as new

Puppies need social contact. Photograph by Lynette Hodge

In the socialisation period the puppy learns to interact with its litter mates – and much more.

Finding out that other dogs are friends.

experiences come along, it learns to deal with them in the safety of the nest and surrounding area. During the early part of this period, it approaches new objects, humans, dogs, other animals and anything that moves with great interest.

Through play, the Leo puppy learns how to control biting, about prey-killing skills, and about acceptable behaviour within the group as a result of interactions within the litter, with the mother, and with other animals and objects that it meets. It learns the consequences of its actions and reactions. It learns dominance and submission, and all the levels between.

Play is a most important part of the development, and animals that play are more highly developed, intelligent and easier to train, because play leads them into various situations which they learn how to deal with. Pups denied play can develop strange behaviours such as self-mutilation; they don't learn as well as they should, are more shy, and reluctant to explore.

Puppies isolated, deprived of sufficient social contact, or having bad experiences during this all-important time can exhibit behaviour that is difficult to deal with in later life, such as fear, hyper-aggression, inhibited behaviour and the inability to learn. They do not learn to inhibit the bite and are difficult to control in many situations. Pups deprived of canine company are very human oriented, and prefer human company to canine. This may seem desirable in some situations, but unfortunately the dog may react in a fearful or aggressive way when it does come into contact with other animals, and often the females make poor mothers.

Breeders should start, and new owners continue, to help the pup, by making sure it is introduced to a wide range of things; for instance, other animals, vacuum cleaners, hair dryers, children, people of both sexes, people in hats, aerosols, umbrellas, different textures and floor coverings, tastes, smells, air changes, temperatures, and much more. It is possible to make the dog so blasé about novel experiences that it reacts well to almost every new and changing situation. Stimuli should not be

New and novel items help to stimulate the pup's mental ability.

introduced in a way that makes the pup fearful, as this is counter-productive, although it is good for the pup to experience and recover from some minor traumas to help it deal with adversity in the future. The pup that is 'wrapped in cotton wool' and only allowed good experiences may develop a different set of behavioural problems. Pups are also influenced by the mother's reaction to various situations. If the bitch is frightened, this is transmitted to the puppies and they, too, are affected.

The Juvenile Period
Overlapping the socialisation period, the juvenile period starts at about 10–12 weeks and stretches to the emergence of sexual maturity. During this time, the pup practises and perfects its motor skills, learns what behaviours to use and where, and the relevance or effect of that behaviour on a particular situation. It learns and develops its position in the hierarchy. At approximately 10 weeks, the ability to learn is nearly fully developed, but by 12 weeks the influence of what the pup has already learnt slows down its ability to take in new tasks. The concentration span of the juvenile dog is much shorter than the adult's, and needs to be developed before more difficult tasks can be taught.

Males learn to raise or 'cock' their leg to urinate and this marks the end of the juvenile period. The timing of this depends on the individual and is often quite late in low-ranking animals. Males mature slowly and it is an on-going procedure with the amount of testosterone (male hormone responsible for male behaviour, and the production of sperm) gradually increasing. The young male Leo becomes interested in on-heat bitches as early as four months of age, but cannot have a fertile mating until around seven to eight months.

During the juvenile period, position in the hierarchy is developed...

... and social skills are explored.

A female has a much more sudden change from juvenile to young adult, usually coinciding with the first season, and therefore the timing depends on the bitch as an individual. Some bitches have their first season (oestrus), at about six months. Others can be as old as 18 months before they cycle.

Adolescence

Adolescence is a period in the dog's life sometimes neglected from the point of view of its importance as a life stage. It is the period when the dog is becoming a sexually-mature young adult with a juvenile's mind. Many owners experience the results of the out-of-control teenager, when their cuddly teddy bear turns into a hooligan overnight. They desperately reach out to every dog trainer, behavioural consultant and vet in their efforts to gain control of the beast. Often the dog displays angelic qualities in the hands of others, but is a real problem with the owner and at home. Some owners take this personally or cannot cope with the situation. This is one of the most common times when dogs are re-homed. The problem does not happen overnight; there is a gradual build-up, and the Leo's maturing body and mind must be controlled and stimulated effectively if the dog is to remain under the owner's control.

The significance of body stance becomes more apparent.

In order for you to survive this stage of your Leo's development, it is important to acknowledge its existence. The key is to give your dog sufficient stimulation to occupy both mind and body, rendering it fulfilled. In the wild, the dog would be out practising its newly-acquired hunting skills, or working on its powers of seduction and status building. In the domestic situation, it has learnt the basics of life, so what now? It needs to have more to do than hang around waiting for something to happen.

Even if you have been vigilant and followed a training programme, your Leo may hit adolescence and become a raving nutcase – or worse! At the onset of early puppy training the dog is over-awed by this strange world in which it finds itself, and looks to you for guidance. With the onset of puberty, evolution decrees that the youngster becomes more independent and ready to deal with life alone. Now there is a conflict between the young body and mind and the restraints of those who set the rules!

Survive your Leo's adolescence and you are set for life! Alamo, photographed by Pam Wells/Travelling Light

The adolescent Leonberger finds it very difficult to concentrate. It is bigger, stronger, and life holds so much in store that it is a bore being tied to mother's apron strings. In order to maintain control, you must do more than merely follow a series of training exercises and social training. The dog needs to know that you are in control, and still look to you for guidance and security. This control cannot be shown by aggression, but by the way you create and manipulate situations to go the right way. We do not want the Leonberger to grow up taking control of its own life, because it needs to live as part of ours.

Adulthood

Leonbergers do not become fully mature until they are two to three years old, and males tend to mature later rather than sooner.

With the onset of maturity, many dogs again go through a rather difficult stage (for their owners, that is). They become more independent, more powerful, more focused. Once again it is essential that training and control are in evidence at this stage. Males are sometimes more of a handful than females, but both can be a challenge to even a knowledgeable handler. Increasing dominance is one of the most common problems and rules should be observed to control this (see page 149 onwards).

It is not impossible to train an older dog, and sometimes the older, more mature dog responds more quickly to an experienced handler than a puppy. It should be remembered, however, that once a behaviour is learned, it does not

The young adult finds it difficult to concentrate and, if not guided correctly, can develop problem behaviours.

simply go away following training. It can be over-trained (an alternative behaviour taught), or extinguished (not allowed to occur or not rewarded when it does), but the underlying behaviour is always there and can surface given the right (or wrong) set of circumstances.

Owning a Leonberger of any age is a joy and certainly attracts attention. However, we must not forget that it is a very large, very powerful dog with canine instincts and motivations. Therefore, training and basic control should be on-going and never laid aside under the belief that the dog is ever fully trained. Left to its own devices, any dog (whatever the breed), makes choices that may not coincide with your own or the general public's, and problems can occur. With any large dog, the uninitiated point the finger before asking questions, and behaviours that might be laughed at or dismissed as cute in smaller breeds are seen as a serious problem in a large breed like the Leonberger. Therefore you owe it to this most majestic of breeds to make sure that you are in full control 100% of the time.

Owning a Leonberger can be a joy. Angela White and Willow meet TV Vet, John Baxter.

The First Few Weeks

The best age to get your Leonberger puppy is at about seven to eight weeks because this gives it time to adjust to you, your family and the new environment when it is still very much a baby, and in the socialisation period of its development. If you get a puppy older than this, you are cutting down the time that you have to socialise it before it enters the period in its development which causes it to be more fearful and less adaptable.

Assuming your pup is from a reputable breeder, its mother will have been inoculated before she became pregnant and passed on some of this immunity to her babies.

Most veterinarians advise that you should not take the pup out until it is fully inoculated, and allow a couple of weeks after this to be on the safe side. Unfortunately, this timing coincides with the most important few weeks of the pup's life with you, and it needs to have as many stimulating and worldly experiences as possible in order to develop and become a normal, intelligent and well-adjusted dog.

Therefore you must look for ways to protect all aspects of your Leo's health, both physical and

The best age to get your pup, from a social point of view, is when it is seven to eight weeks old.

mental. Many things can be done with, and introduced to, the pup without subjecting it to increased risk of disease, or at least keeping this to a minimum.

Socialising at Home

Your Leo pup needs to learn about other humans, so invite children and older people to visit and allow controlled interaction. Do not let your pup get over-excited in these situations because it is going to grow very large, and what seems cute from a fluffy teddy bear can be a positive nightmare from a 88kg (14 stone) hooligan.

Investigating the garden is a tiring business. Photograph by Lynette Hodge

Do not shelter the pup from household appliances, such as the vacuum cleaner or hairdryer. Try to get someone else to do the vacuum cleaning to start with, while you hold the pup and give it confidence. (What a good excuse to get someone else to do the house work: 'Sorry, I'm training my Leo'!)

Objects that the pup has not seen before might make it 'spook', so try to find different things to put in the garden or kitchen which the pup can investigate at its own pace and with your support. Pups also need to know about different sounds and aromas. Sudden bangs and strong smells can unsettle the puppy, so introduce them in the safety of your own home and garden. Encourage the puppy to explore, search for handkerchiefs or hidden toys, teach it simple exercises and even a few tricks. The more you stimulate its senses and brain, the more well-adjusted, adaptable and easy to train it will be.

The Big Outdoors

If your pup is still small enough to carry, take it into the big outdoors without its feet coming into contact with the contaminated pathways and roads. It will learn much under your protective arm, and understand which noises, smells, and sights are not to be feared. This cannot last long with a Leonberger, as it puts on weight very quickly and soon becomes too heavy to carry.

You can take the pup to visit dog-free households, or where you know the dogs are 'pup friendly', fully inoculated, and not allowed to go into high-risk areas. Be careful if at any time your pup has to come into contact with public areas; do not let it sniff around or go into areas that are obviously dirty and keep any contact to an absolute minimum.

It is also a good idea to introduce your pup to animals that you don't have at home. Early, controlled experience of horses, cattle, sheep, cats and poultry can

An introduction to livestock in a controlled environment is valuable learning.

save anguish later, and is preferable to trying to hang on to a fully grown Leo who has suddenly discovered and taken a dislike (or even an obsessive like) to one of the above.

Travelling in the Car

Take your Leo pup out in the car as often as possible, even before it is inoculated, as this is an extension to your home. In most cases Leonbergers travel well, being content to settle down into a snooze until the engine stops, especially if you take care not to feed them immediately before a journey, and give them the security of a human to reassure them.

It is best if the pup travels in the back of the car and, eventually, it should travel behind a dog guard or in a crate for security. If the pup is in the front, it should be on the floor in the well and not on the seat by the driver, as this is very distracting, potentially dangerous and, in some countries, illegal.

You can start by training your Leo to travel on the back seat with you, to get it used to the car, but eventually it will have to travel in the back on its own. Whether you are training a pup or an adult, the procedure is the same, by teaching good associations. The average Leonberger, after a couple of excursions with you on the back seat, will quite happily settle there alone while you sit with the driver in the front. It is a simple step from here to teaching the Leo to be in the far back of the car, but help the dog to understand by following these steps:

Step One With the car stationary, feed the Leo in the back. Sit with it with the back door open. Stroke it and keep it calm.
Step Two Teach the pup to lie down in the back by doing the 'down' exercise as described on page 181.

Step Three Gently close the car door for a few seconds, and then open it again and reward the pup calmly. Slowly increase the time the door is closed, and give the pup something to occupy itself, such as a chew or titbit.

Step Four When you are confident that the pup is settled, start the engine but keep the car stationary. Return to the back and make sure the pup is happy, and repeat the above stages with the engine running.

Step Five When the pup is confident with steps one to four, drive a very short distance. If it has shown no signs of travel sickness on previous journeys give a chew stick to keep it occupied.

By now you should be well on with the training of the essential control exercises (see Chapter 12) so you will be able to use your keyword for 'Down' to keep your dog under control.

It is safer if the pup lies down while the car is moving. Most pups automatically lie down on the first journey as this is a submissive position, and they do not wish to antagonise anyone in a situation that they are unsure of. Later, they may try to stand up but you should try to keep them down, as this also helps to avoid travel sickness. Travel sickness is often caused by the dog watching the movement out of the window. Excitable or anxious dogs become more so if they are allowed to stand and watch, so gently and calmly persevere in keeping the pup down.

Most Leos need to learn about travelling in cars, so the earlier, the better.

If you do not have an estate or hatchback car, then a doggy travel harness might be a good investment as the dog matures. This helps to secure safely the dog to the seatbelt, and prevents it from wandering around. The more journeys your Leo goes on, the more it will come to understand and enjoy the experience. Many well-trained dogs are keen to get into the car rather than avoid it.

Setting the Rules

Even before your Leonberger comes to your home, you should have decided what rules are to be observed for both the dog and the rest of the family. All households have rules, some to do with the social structure and some more practical. Your new Leonberger will come into your household and run riot if no rules have been thought out, set and put into practice.

The Leonberger cannot understand the concept of 'muddy' or 'wet' and, believe me, there is nothing as muddy as a muddy Leo! So when it runs in from the garden with dirty paws and you try to explain the error of its ways, it is at a loss to understand a word. It may understand from your tone, body language and attitude that you are not pleased, but why? The dog has no idea.

You must set rules and abide by them so that your Leo knows where it stands. Create a routine that avoids problems. For instance, do not let your Leo straight into your best room when it comes in from outside, whatever the weather. Do not let the dog onto furniture without an invitation. Never allow it to jump up, and so on. Whatever behaviours you think could cause problems should be put under control before you go any further.

It is a good idea to restrict your Leo's access.

Access in the house

Some common behavioural problems occur when dogs are allowed free access to all areas of the house. Apart from possible damage, there is the issue of dominance. If you have no areas of your home that are exclusive to humans, your Leo may decide that it is on the same level in the heirarchy as all the humans. Should you want it out of the way, at some point it may challenge your authority in the only way it knows, by growling or, worse still, biting.

Therefore, make rules from the start. Decide on areas where your Leo can go in any circumstance, or that can be blocked if the need arises. For instance, my dogs are allowed in the kitchen and hallway from the garden while I am present, because these areas are easily cleaned, and there is little chance of damage. All other areas have their doors closed and the dogs cannot gain free access. They come into those other rooms only on my invitation.

Allowing your Leo to share your bed is not a good idea. If you wish to remain top dog you must protect your sleeping area.

If at all possible, have a reasonably-sized area in which the dog can be enclosed when you are out of the house or very busy, or if it comes in wet or muddy. If you are out for long periods at a time, even if this is only occasionally, then an outside area is essential. If you leave your Leo only for short periods, then an indoor enclosure or designated dog room suffices. By creating a safe area you are doing yourself and the dog a favour. The dog appreciates a place of its own where it is safe, and you do not come home to chewed-up furniture or mess in the house.

Bedrooms are another cause of much anguish and soul-seeking. A dominant dog should never be allowed in the bedroom and, more especially, never on the bed. If you want to remain at the top of the pack, you must be sure to maintain your individual bed area and not allow the dog to share or, worse still, have free access to it. If you wish to have your dog in the bedroom, take it with you, make it wait outside the room if you go into the bathroom and, after you are in the room, call it in and make it lie by the side of the bed on the floor, or on its own bed at floor level. If your Leo shows any sign of growling or dominant body stance, stop even this privilege immediately. If you allow this to go on, even the sweetest of Leos may get 'ideas above its station', and you will end up with problems that are very difficult for you to deal with and may result in you having to get rid of the dog. It is most disturbing to have the once-pleasant face of your pet growling and snarling on top of you while you lie in bed, and it will be your own fault if you do not set the rules now – and stick to them! You may think that this will not happen to you, and that your sweet, cuddly puppy would never be like that; many new owners feel this way and ignore advice but six months to a year later are extremely upset by their dog's apparently abnormal, but in reality quite normal, dominant behaviour.

Some Leo owners never experience problems and, indeed, I have seen a car sticker which says 'Keep warm – go to bed with a Leo'. In my experience, they take up too much room.

Always make your Leo do something for you before it is fed.

Feeding Time

Feeding and table manners also need their own set of rules. Start as you mean to go on; do not allow scrounging from the table, or allow family and friends to throw titbits to your Leo. Feed it only on its own dishes, in an open area so that it is difficult for it to guard its food, do not always feed in exactly the same spot, and always make the pup do something like 'Sit', or 'Down', before it is fed.

Feeding time is ideal to practise training techniques, because you have your Leo's full attention, and it will be very keen to please. This also gives you a much higher level of mental control over the dog, and it will be less likely to challenge your authority when it knows you control its food.

If you want your Leo on the furniture it should be by your invitation only. Bridie tries her luck.

Furniture

Whether or not to let the pup on the furniture is another dilemma. The pup does not know when it has dirty paws, and the dominance rule also applies as an elevated position is a position of power. Therefore teach the dog to come onto the furniture only when invited (see page 188).

Doorways

It is important that your Leonberger does not barge through doorways. The sheer size of the adult animal is reason enough – even if you are reasonably fit, the results can be disastrous if the dog pushes past. And, once again, the dominance rule applies. The dog in charge of the pack goes through gaps first to investigate the other side. This must be you! (See page 200 for rules on training this behaviour.)

Biting or Mouthing

Most puppies bite or mouth your hand, especially when they are young and going through the teething period. This can be very painful as the teeth are needle sharp. Biting and mouthing is a very natural behaviour, because the dog finds out about its environment with its mouth, and has to learn how hard it may or may not bite. But you must draw the line somewhere. Allow the dog to start a little mouthing on your arm, but not too much, and when it begins to get too excited, immediately withdraw and say 'No'. Show your Leo that you are hurt and that you no longer want to play; ignore its attention. Once it has backed off, invite it to play, this time introducing a good-sized tugger toy. Encourage it to bite this, but if it catches your skin, immediately withdraw and stop the game. Again show by your attitude and body language that you are hurt, and you no longer want to play.

Most Leo puppies want to play, and therefore very soon learn to play on your terms. Children are very good at teaching this because their skin is more tender and they tolerate less bites before withdrawing. But do not put young children at risk of getting hurt; first train the dog yourself.

Many people are tempted to tap the dog's nose or smack it when it bites. Probably, the dog will not respond in the desired manner, often thinking that this is all part of the game and you are playing rough, so it joins in the fun and plays rough too. If you shout, it can be noisy too, so this increases the pup's excitement. You must remember that the puppy is only playing puppy games and, unless you teach it your rules in a way that it can understand, it will use its own set of rules.

Digging

Leonbergers love to dig; digging is a natural behaviour, it is what dogs do and, Leos being Leos, they do it bigger and better than most. The best way to control this activity is to provide them with a place where they can dig, and encourage them to do so.

Teach your Leo to play with a tug toy instead of your hands but remember, you must be in control of the games.

But how do you get your Leo to differentiate between your idea of a 'good' place and your favourite flower bed? One patch of ground and vegetation looks pretty much the same as another to a Leonberger.

The art is to make the 'good' place irresistible to your Leo. Bury hidden treasure in the form of a bone, a toy, a biscuit, or whatever your Leo likes best, in its own special digging pit. Then take it out on a lead to this area, encourage it to dig and help it find the prize. Continue to bury more treasure over a period of time until you reach the stage where the dog is desperate to get to its digging pit to hit 'Leo gold'. After a while, digging in other less productive areas loses its appeal. You are happy, and your digging Leo is happy.

Toys

All puppies should have safe toys which can serve as great training aids. However, there is a danger that your Leo will start to rule your life with its toys. At first this is very subtle, and you do not notice it happening. You encourage the dog to play, and it discovers that when it brings the toys to you, you play with it. Sounds cute, doesn't it? A special area for the toys may have been allocated, a toy box or even the dog's bed, and you tidy up, collecting all the toys and putting them together. Some dogs start to become possessive over these toys and you may hear the odd growl, or the signal may be as subtle as a dominant body posture over the toys. When you ignore this, the dog interprets it as a win, and so takes another step up the ladder to top dog position. This behaviour is potentially dangerous, and someone will end up by getting bitten.

The correct way to play is for you to maintain the control of the toys and, if you play games with your Leo, you must end up with ultimate possession of the toy. Do not enter into games that you may not win. At the end of the game (and you decide on when the end will be, don't wait for the dog to tire), put the toys away out of the pup's reach.

The toys are your toys, and your Leo is allowed to play with them at your discretion. You might feel that the dog should win some games but, if you want to maintain mental and physical control, I suggest you heed this advice. Your dog will win many advantages through its life, which you will not even be aware of so, whenever you can, actively do something to lower its position in the hierarchy with the humans.

Another advantage is that the toys become a great training aid. Because the Leo does not have free access to the toys they are interesting and fun, and it associates them with having fun with you. That is a good basis for working on your relationship with the pup.

A special toy in your pocket when you go out together is a great asset because, whenever you want the dog back, you can bring out the toy and your Leo will be keen to come back and play with you. If you call, and it sees this as the end of its fun, your Leo is far less likely to want to come back, and this is the start of one of the most common behavioural problems, 'My dog won't come back when he is called'. Start as you mean to go on and you will never have this problem.

Going to the Vet

One of the first visits your Leo pup experiences is to the veterinary surgeon for a check up and perhaps an inoculation. This can be traumatic, but you can play a big part in making the visit as pleasant as possible. Unless you are worried about some aspect of your pup's health, allow it a couple of days to settle in and to build up its confidence in you.

A good vet takes time to say 'Hello'.

Practise lifting and putting the pup on a table, because this is what will happen at the surgery. Hold it safely against your body, put your arm around the pup and reassure it and, as it starts to settle, give a reward. Do this two or three times a day. Give a keyword, such as 'Table', to associate with this new lesson. Soon the pup will be quite happy with this new experience, and it will be one less for it to have to comprehend when it goes to the vet. Once the pup is confident, try to bring it into the stand position (see page 183).

Try to arrange a quiet time for the appointment so that there are not too many other dogs around. Write down any questions you may have as it is easy to forget what you had to say when you get into the surgery. Carry some treats for your pup. If you can avoid it, that is, if the pup is light enough to carry, do not put it on the floor in the waiting room as many sick animals will have been there and the risk of infection is high even in the cleanest of places. If your pup is too large to carry and hold on your lap, leave it in the car with a friend, or ask the receptionist to call you when it is your turn to go in. Do not introduce your pup to other dogs, because dogs at the surgery probably are there because they are ill and stressed, not the best frame of mind for meeting puppies.

When you enter the surgery, put your Leo on the table, just as you did at home, and keep a supportive arm around it. Offer a treat and, even if it does not take it, the familiar sight and smell help to relax the pup a little. A good vet will take time to say 'Hello' to the pup and build its confidence before starting the examination and will even have a supply of treats. In my experience, most vets are interested in the Leonberger as it is not the sort of dog they see every day.

Talk to the pup soothingly during the examination. The vet may want to take the pup's temperature, which means that he will insert a thermometer into your Leo's anus. Most pups do not worry about this too much, but do need to be standing, so once again your training comes into its own. Other tests may include testing the heart rate, checking ears, mouth, eyes, and feeling the abdomen and checking testicles. Then comes the inoculation. Hold the pup as directed by the vet, normally sideways on but with head facing you, and soothe it with your voice, stroking it all the while. The vet inoculates into the very loose skin between the back of the neck and the pup's shoulders and, with any luck, the pup won't even notice. Reward it again, and ask the vet to fuss it, especially if the pup did feel the needle. It is important that the pup is not unduly frightened by the experience, so take as much time as the vet will allow.

Most puppies come out from their first visit to the veterinary surgeon with a clean bill of health. Listen carefully to what you are told, and if in doubt ask for an explanation, and don't be afraid to discuss any problems – you are paying for this, remember. If you have not been given worming tablets for the pup from your breeder, get some from the vet. They will be suitable and effective, and take away any uncertainty you may have of buying them over the counter at a pet shop.

Veterinary nurses always like to cuddle new puppies, and a cuddly Leo pup in the surgery is a pleasant experience for them, so make the most of the whole visit by allowing them time to make your Leo's acquaintance. The vet nurse is also one of the best people to ask about the availability of puppy groups and training classes in your area.

Grooming

Grooming is a very important social activity. All Leos need to be groomed, but this should not be left until it is obvious that the dog is in need of a good brushing. The pup should be groomed regularly and its whole body checked over so that, when it has to be examined, it makes no objection. When grooming your Leo, be sure to get down to the skin as it is very easy to surface groom, that is, groom only the top coat. The Leonberger has a dense undercoat, and this must be groomed thoroughly to make the dog feel comfortable and to avoid harbouring skin pests and foreign bodies. Good quality grooming also helps to keep your Leo cool, by removing all the dead hair that otherwise can mat and form a barrier so that air cannot get to the skin. An uncomfortable dog may become an irritable dog, so grooming is an important preventative therapy.

This is a good time to pay attention to your Leo's feet and to check its mouth. At first it may not like to be handled here, so take things slowly, and have a handful of titbits to keep it happy. Don't worry about actually doing the inspection or clipping the claws to start with. Go through the motions, praising and rewarding your pup as you go along.

It is best to do the grooming on a table with a pup, or a raised platform with an older dog, as this prevents the back-breaking pain that comes from stooping over your dog. Also, the Leo is more inclined to conform if it gets used to a specific place for this procedure.

Puppy Parties and Play Groups

Many forward-thinking veterinary surgeons now organise puppy parties or play groups to bring together families and their puppies, to help with social skills, to advise on the behavioural aspects of the pup's well-being and also on basic health care. Sometimes these are run by the vet or veterinary nurse, or a behavioural trainer is invited to take the class, and sometimes it is a combination of the two. These gatherings should be constructive. The puppies are allowed a certain amount of freedom but are not allowed to have a free-for-all, where they might learn aggressive or inappropriate behaviours.

Visitors

Every household has at least three different types of visitor: friends or family who come regularly, friends/family who come on rarer occasions, and those who deliver items or give services such as postmen/women, window cleaners and refuse collectors. The Leo pup needs to understand that all these people are allowed to call, and should not be feared, barked at or attacked. When the pup is very young it is relatively easy to control but, as it becomes more confident, it may become a little out of hand.

The best method is to introduce the pup to any visitors on a lead and in a controlled situation, particularly if it is the boisterous type. The last thing you want is a happy-go-lucky pup bounding all over an unsuspecting visitor and being shouted at or even smacked. Faced with a dog, even a young pup, bounding towards them many people panic, scream and wave their arms about. All this excites or startles the dog even more, and it may jump up to try to grab at those things waving around! The more sensitive Leo learns that people are to be feared, and later this can lead to aggression caused by fear. The next time your Leo sees the visitor, the whole situation will be ten times worse. The pup will be more excited and the person will respond even sooner in a desperate attempt to avoid the confrontation.

The solution is to think ahead and set up situations so that you can have full control. Do not allow the dog free access to the entrance of your garden or yard where visitors might enter unannounced and startle your Leo. The dog should be introduced to the visitor on lead, and told to sit while the visitor gives it a titbit.

One of the best things to do is to have a small 'Leo welcoming party'. Have some treats ready and tell your guests to collect a titbit for the puppy on the way in. Often you will have to instruct your visitors how to behave around your puppy. Many people bury their heads in the cuddly Leo's fur, or bend over the animal. If the puppy is a little nervous this will make it worse. Tell people to stand or sit up straight, and not to bend over the animal.

Another common action is for people to stare straight into the animal's eyes. This is very unnerving for the dog, so watch for the people who do this and explain that this action is seen by the dog as an act of confrontational dominance and not something that should be done to any animal. The pup should not be allowed to lick people's faces; it's amazing how many visitors seem happy to allow this to happen.

Leos must learn not to pester the visitors. Rosso and Timja practise their lesson.

Do not allow your Leonberger to pester anyone unduly. It must learn that it is all right to say 'Hello' in a controlled manner, but then it must lie down, or come back to your side where you can control its behaviour.

Child visitors are often a problem because they want to play with the puppy, and at this stage you may not have been able to teach the puppy to play gently. The only way to avoid problems is to control both child and puppy. Allow a small amount of supervised play, showing the child how to play. Make sure that the child does not roll around on the floor with the pup, as this give the pup the idea that it is equal to, if not higher ranking than, the child. Be constructive and show the child how to train the puppy with titbits. Soon the child will be able to get the pup to go into the sit, down, and stand and maybe even follow at heel.

If you have a quieter, more sensitive pup, leave it to come out when it is ready. Encourage it out gently by putting some food nearby or rolling a toy around the floor. Avoid a direct confrontation and eye to eye contact because the dog will take this as a sign that you are exerting dominance over it, or confronting it in a dominant way. The sensitive, more submissive pup is probably

The better you know your Leo, the better will be your relationship.

quite happy to accept your control without you adding any more power to it!

Getting to Know your Leo

The better you are at understanding everything about your new Leonberger puppy, the better relationship you will have, and the better control you will be able to display.

Getting to know your dog is not just about learning when it is going to misbehave, but about knowing every little mood and action. In my experience, the best way to do this is to spend as much time as possible with it, and make sure that much of that time is, as it is termed nowadays, 'quality time'.

These sessions should be instigated by you, so the pup does not get the idea that it can demand attention at any time. Sit with it in front of you (on the floor with very young pups), or on a low seat if you feel more comfortable, and stroke, touch and even gently massage its body. Stroke the mouth, head, the legs right down to the feet, between the pads, inner thighs, and the tail from base to tip. Make sure that every part of its body

New experiences all help to build your pups' character.

can be touched and, with gentle slow movements, teach the dog that your attentions are kind and enjoyable. Move your hands in gentle, circular, soothing movements; your dog may find it a little odd to start with, but persevere as this helps it to relax and make it more aware of its own body. When your pup is teething, massage its gums, just as you might a baby. These sessions not only help the pup to relax, but they will also help you to relax with your dog.

Attention Seeking

Now that your Leonberger is discovering you are to be trusted, it may start to become a little over-demanding, and pester you or other family members for attention. This often happens, perhaps surprisingly, with people who are not at home with the pup all the time. When someone comes home from work, college or school, the Leo will rush to see them and the most likely response is one of affection. You must be careful that this does not progress into the pup demanding and getting attention regularly, as the next step from this is a dominance struggle.

Therefore it is important that your Leo learns that humans do not respond every time it approaches, and that it must do something for the human before the human responds to the pup's request. Make sure that all the family follows this rule, especially children. Each member of the family should make the dog regularly (at least every other time), go and lie down instead of pestering them, and then make sure the dog has settled or is distracted before they respond to its needs.

A more submissive Leo can be afforded more privileges but, as the pup approaches adolescence, you should withdraw and restrict some of these privileges just to make sure it knows where it stands in the social structure of the household.

Always in Trouble!

Sometimes Leo puppies become adventurous, and you may have difficulty stopping inappropriate behaviour. In these cases it is useful to attach a house lead to your Leo's collar, made from cheap, light-weight rope or line, about 1.6–3m (6–10ft) long. The lead trails behind the Leo so you can get hold of it more easily, reel it in and put it under immediate control, thus making sure that the dog behaves correctly. If it chews the line just tie a knot in it and don't worry. However, you should not leave the line attached to the pup if you are not with it, in case it gets tangled.

This long line can also very useful if your Leo decides that it is more fun to run away than to come back to you when out for a walk (see Chapter 12, page 189). Gradually you will be able to dispense with the line, but it serves as a remote extension to your arm, and helps to give you the confidence to train and control with a pleasant attitude.

What a temptation, even for the best-trained dog!

A safe place to dig – with no danger to the geraniums!

'Mad Half Hour'

The owners of many Leonbergers suffer from their puppies' 'mad half hours'. In reality the session often lasts only a few minutes, but it sometimes feels like half an hour! The Leo puts back its ears and races at top speed around tables, chairs, people, the cat, the kitchen, into the garden and then, just for good measure, does another lap or two! There are various reasons for this behaviour. Sometimes it is pent-up energy, as it often occurs in the evening. Generally it is just a thing that puppies do.

When my pups do it I give a keyword and put it under my control. If you do this, eventually you can instigate the behaviour by attitude and command. If you do not want the behaviour, ignore it. Leo pups (normally) grow out of it. Certainly it is not a good idea to chastise the pup because this just draws attention to the act, and builds up more frustrations.

'Spooky' Leos

As the Leo pup starts to grow up, there may be things that make it 'spook', even after the best social training. An unusual noise, a strange shape in a familiar setting, a sudden movement, or a person, animal, or vehicle coming apparently from nowhere are all things that might make the otherwise normal puppy react, and then what sort of reaction you get depends on its character. It might try to run away or stand its ground, bark, growl, or may chase and snap. Often this behaviour comes as a complete surprise to owners, who blame all sorts of things in their ignorance.

Sometimes the behaviour seems unpredictable, and sometimes it is – to us. Often changes or developments in behaviour of this sort coincide with adolescence. The pup is now growing up and becoming increasingly sensitive to environment and change. We are far less sensitive than the dog and do not always realise what might startle it. Colour can play a part; take the case of the unfortunate jogger. Ignored by the pup previously, today he is wearing bright red – a warning colour in the animal kingdom. Or that same jogger suddenly decides to look the pup straight in the eye – a dominant stare. Previously the pup may have seen only the moving feet but today it sees the eyes and must react. It will react in the instinctive or learned way that comes first to its mind, without stopping to think what might be most appropriate, or what the humans might prefer.

To counteract these particular problems, you must teach your Leo to trust you and to look to you when unfamiliar situations present themselves. Recognising the fact that the pup or young dog is 'spooking' is the most important factor, and the next step is dealing with it in a controlled manner.

In some situations it is appropriate to go up to the object that your Leo is frightened of and show that it is all right. Take your time and encourage it with a treat. Try not to make a big deal out of the whole thing. If it has spooked at an object, simply go and stand by the offending article, pat it, talk to it, ignore your Leo to a degree, and soon the pup will come over and see that there is nothing to be feared. If it does not come to investigate, don't force it, simply walk away and try again tomorrow.

Training Classes

As soon as your pup has had its inoculations it is a good idea to take it to classes. If you are going to show it go to Obedience classes as well as Ringcraft classes. Choose the class carefully, and make sure it has competent instructors who have complete but pleasant control. The last thing you want is for your vulnerable pup to be attacked by another dog and, at the other end of the scale, uncontrolled play can lead to a very boisterous and out-of-control Leonberger. A good class will have an air of calm and pleasant control without any aggression being shown by handlers or instructors. It is a good idea to go along and inspect it without the dog so you can concentrate on the class procedure and assess the quality of teaching before you have to concentrate on your Leonberger.

How to be Top Dog

Leonbergers can be born with or develop dominant tendencies to a lesser or greater degree, depending on the individual and the way in which it is brought up. Dominance is seen more often in dogs than bitches, but owners of females should not breathe a sigh of relief and relax, as bitches can become dominant as well.

How can you recognise a dominant, or potentially dominant, dog? All too often, dog owners only realise, or are told by a professional behavioural counsellor, that they have a dominant dog when its attitude and behaviour has started to get out of hand. A grumble over food or a growl about being moved – the warning signs are there long before the problem takes hold, if only they could be identified by the dog owner before it is too late! Often, dog owners live with certain behaviours on the pretext of having 'a quiet life', but it soon becomes obvious that life is by no means quiet!

Starting out on the correct footing with your Leonberger puppy should mean that you never experience the trauma of living with an out-of-control, dominant dog. If your pup is destined to be dominant then, believe me, it will have a good try at climbing the hierarchy ladder.

Obviously some Leos are more difficult than others. Where a certain line has been selectively bred for domestic or show purposes, some of the more difficult and undesirable tendencies may not be so prominent, but this is not guaranteed. In some cases, the beauty of the dog has been at the forefront of the breeder's mind, and behavioural tendencies ignored or not considered a problem.

Recognising Dominance

Imagine this scene: a harmless Leo pup is lying across a doorway in a typical puppy snooze. You and the family are walking carefully around so as not to disturb it. A sleepy eye opens and the pup is reluctant to move, so you decide to leave it because 'he's tired'. Unknowingly, the pup has just taken its first step on the road to dominance.

Training should be carried out with absolute trust between owner and dog.

Body posture says a lot – what is Jet saying?

A few more similar occurrences and the Leo, who is not a stupid character, starts to assume control of its new-found power. Soon it finds other situations which show it that it is boss.

Typical Scenarios

Following are some typical and very common scenarios to give you a few examples of how the Leo can start to take control.

Eating its meal in a corner You have put it in a quiet corner to eat its meal in peace. In itself, this is not a bad idea. The problem is that the pup sees the quiet corner as an easy place in which to protect its precious dinner. It may growl quietly as a person or another animal passes by, or simply adjust its posture to a more upright, dominant stance. The latter is easy to miss, the former is often dismissed as cute or the pup being just a pup.

Getting its food before the family Again this makes sense to us. It means the pup is fed and settled, and perhaps less likely to pester at the table. With a pup eating several meals a day, it is often difficult to avoid doing this even if you try. However, if this happens regularly, and the dog is never hungry, you will be setting a precedence of hierarchy. He who eats first is in control of the food supply.

Brings its toys and instigates games This is very 'cute' behaviour, and is temptingly easy to encourage. But, as with food, when the dog is controlling things, it is asserting its dominance over the situation. Admittedly, it does not always start out this way, but this is where it may lead.

Has own bed in corner   Again this is a common thing for owners to do, and is often recommended by experts. It is good for the pup to have an area where it can relax and which it can call its own. However, if you do not go in with it or move the bed now and again, it may decide that this area is exclusive to it.

Climbs onto the furniture, pushing its way between people   Another very 'cute' behaviour. Many Leos, despite their size, are allowed on furniture. But you should allow this on your invitation only, not on your Leo's whim or demand.

The number of inadvertent, dominance-building occurrences are endless. Some people whom I have assisted as a behavioural consultant have had a litany of 'little happenings' that mounted up and culminated in the dog having no doubt that it was the top dog in the family.

Some situations can be much more subtle than those that I have illustrated, and are not always easy to spot. Dominance can become circumstantial or be targeted on specific people. For instance, a member of the household is out a lot, but responds to the dog enthusiastically when he or she come home. This person feels sorry for the dog or is flattered by its attentions, and therefore panders to the dog's advances. The pup learns to single this person out for special attention, and learns that it can control this human's behaviour. Watch this person and the pup interacting. If the person looks directly at the pup – does the pup avert its eyes? It should! Does the pup lick the person excessively? It should not. Does the pup single out this individual as a target to get titbits when the person is eating? It probably does – but it shouldn't. If the pup sees that every member of the family ranks higher than itself, it should not single out individuals for behaviours such as these.

If, on the other hand, the dog simply likes to be around a particular person, then this is quite normal. This usually will be the person who exerts the most control in its life. The dog respects and feels comfortable knowing its place with this person.

Some dogs can be allowed all the scenarios listed above and more, and never be a problem to their owners. Often this is because the dog is not of a dominant nature or because other situations tip the balance and the dog accepts its place. But given enough of the right situations, most dogs can become dominant to some degree, even if the dominance shows or is a problem only in certain situations.

Body posture tells a great deal about your Leo. Dominance is often initially shown with a subtle change in posture from the usual relaxed look to a more exaggerated, very upright stance. Ear set lifts and is pushed forward, the back may arch to give the appearance of being larger. It may even display piloerection (hackles up) at the front end of its body. If the dog is guarding something, then its head may be lowered towards the item but its face will be turned towards you. In the early stages there may be no more than these subtle body posture changes, and this is one of the reasons why dominance goes unnoticed until it has reached the next stage. Then the dog shows actual aggression when it feels its dominance is being challenged, or to get what it wants.

Chapter 11

Understanding Dominance

All animals (and domestic dogs are no different), live with two basic motivations, food and sex: in other words, self-preservation and perpetuating the species. Being top of the hierarchy is part of the pattern of life that helps to ensure that your genes are the ones that are passed on. If you are in control of situations then you have the first chance to be in the right place at the right time.

None of this should apply to a pet dog in a household situation, but unfortunately we are unable to explain this to the dog. In its behaviour, the dog reacts very much like a juvenile wolf, with some individuals being born with more built-in programming for potential dominance than others.

Your Leo reacts to situations *as they happen*. Its memory is different from ours in that it does not think laterally as we do, but reacts through instinct or learnt behaviour to the current situation. Therefore we cannot be justified in chastising or rewarding behaviour that has happened earlier, even by only seconds, because the dog has no idea to what you are referring unless your actions coincide with its own, exactly as they happen.

However, we can build up a pattern of behaviour in our dog that informs its instincts that it is no longer in control, and this helps it to understand that taking the dominant role is not such a good idea. We can assert dominance ourselves without ever raising hand or voice to the dog. Handled with aggression, your Leo will react to your actions because it feels threatened. We must rise above the basic urge to control with physical strength and take a much more supreme role to ensure that the Leo does not start or continue to challenge our authority or that of family and friends.

Aggression from you or others is not the answer. The developing Leo sees aggression as a sign that the owner has lost or is losing control, and therefore challenges a little harder or a little sooner next time its behaviour is triggered in the hope that you will be knocked from your shaky pedestal. You may be a powerful person and the dog may not feel that it can challenge you; if this is the case, it may be more inclined to challenge other family members or acquaintances whom it considers lower in the pecking order. If it cannot hit out at its oppressor it will, like humans who are mistreated, hit out at those who are easier targets. This is an instinctive behaviour, not thought out, and relieves the mental pressure built up inside.

Controlling Dominance

Following the guidelines below will help if you have a dominant or potentially-dominant Leonberger. If it is already showing signs of dominance, a marked difference in the dog's behaviour will be observed. Often the differences show within 24 hours of the owner 'seeing the light'. The dog automatically learns by your actions that its place is far down the hierarchy and the chances of a challenge lessen continually whilst you continue to follow the rules strictly. The more controlled you and your family are, the more successful you will be. If your Leo is already showing aggressive dominance to you or any family member, then you must be very strict with yourself in the way that you follow the rules and, if necessary, seek professional counselling.

Rule One   Do not lie on the floor or furniture and allow the pup to lie on you. Take the dominant role by remaining above your Leo both physically and mentally. If you do allow the dog on top of you, an animal with dominant tendencies will feel very much in control.

Rule Two   Take all the Leo's toys and keep them out of its reach in a drawer or cupboard. These must now remain in your possession. Do not feel that you are being mean or depriving the dog, because you make up for this amply with your attention to training and control. Your Leo's life will soon become more fulfilled than ever it was before, because in order to control it, and keep it under control, you have to work hard.

Rule Three   Games must be instigated by you, not the Leo. Only play when you want to, when you feel in control, and when the dog obviously knows that you started the game. Your Leo must not believe that it started the game, even if you feel that it did not; do not cheat on yourself. You must win all the games.

Rule Four   Do not throw toys and allow your Leo to take possession of them. Play should be enjoyed with the dog on lead under your complete control. If the dog should win accidentally, bring it back to you by finding some form of reward that it likes even more than the toy. Always have something in your pocket to aid you in control. Encourage the dog to sit, go down or do another control exercise for the reward and then you have regained control.

Rule Five   If you are playing tug games use a titbit together with the keyword 'Leave' to get your Leo to release on command. Avoid tug games until you know you can win.

Rule Six   Do not allow your Leo to become obsessive over games that it might like to play on its own. Discourage any repetitive or stereotypic actions by distracting it onto other things. Stereotypic behaviour sometimes can be seen in some zoo animals, where normal behaviours become repetitive, seemingly-meaningless actions, often heightened by excitement and frustration. Animals need plenty of stimulating activities and varying environments to prevent this behaviour. Allowing a dominant dog to continue with this behaviour often results in aggression when its drive is interrupted.

Rule Seven   Do not allow your Leo to stare at you eye to eye. If it has this tendency, make it look away before you do by distracting it with your hand or a toy. Then ignore it, act naturally and do not instigate a stare out if it can be avoided.

Rule Eight   Do not allow your dog to demand attention for any reason, even to attend to its bodily functions such as food or toilet. You should anticipate its needs and organise events so that you can make it do something else, or so that it is busy doing something else when you tell it that it is time for toilet, food, and so on.

Rule Nine   Do not position your Leo's bed in an area that it can guard easily. If it displays guarding or dominance tendencies over the bed, call it out of the room the first few times that you move the bed, to avoid confrontation. Make sure that the dog allows you to go freely into its bed area and do this at least several times a day.

Rule Ten   Do not allow the dog free access to your bed area, to the entrance to your bedroom, or even to the hall or landing leading to your bed. Top dogs have an exclusive bed area, so make sure yours is exclusive to you. The Leo's bed area should be available to all the family.

Rule Eleven   Do not allow the pup to barge through doorways ahead of you. This may mean restricting access for the dog until you have trained the appropriate exercise (see page 200). Top dogs inspect the surroundings first; make sure you are top dog.

Rule Twelve   Top dogs make it obvious to their pack that they have the option of eating first. Feed your Leo after you and your family have eaten. If this is not always possible, make sure the dog sees you eating something while you are preparing its meal, even if you pretend to eat the dog food. If the dog has been fed before the family, put it in another room or outside so that it does not watch you eat while it sits there with a full stomach. This also makes it aware that your eating area is exclusive to you.

Rule Thirteen   Do not allow your Leo to eat in a corner of a room. You may need to change the room where it is fed if its food dominance is getting out of hand. This gives you fresh ground and the leading stance.

Rule Fourteen   Teach your Leo that you are in control of food by following this simple training procedure. Prepare the food in a bowl. Offer a morsel of food on a small dish separately, keeping control of the main dish. When the first offering is eaten with no growling or aggression, offer another piece. Continue this process until all the meal is eaten. Bringing the dish back and replenishing it teaches the dog that you are more likely to give more food than to take it away. If there are any signs of growling or aggression, withdraw and offer no more food. Try again later. You may find better control if you change the room where you feed and put the dog under the control of its lead. The Leonberger soon learns that you are in control of the food and that you offer more food when it responds correctly. Once you are confident, allow the dog a little more food at a time and alternate this with putting the dish on the floor. Keep up this procedure of control at each meal until you and every member of the family, including children, are completely confident. It is important that the dog sees that all the family are above it in the hierarchy, but do not put your children at risk of being bitten; make sure that you are in complete control of the dog first, and control your children. Make sure the dog is aware that you are backing the children. Ask the child to watch you first and then stand immediately behind him or her to guide and give confidence. Do not get cross with the child, as the dog may think it is its duty to help you (the top dog) to chastise the underling (child).

Rule Fifteen   Train your Leonberger using the techniques described in Chapter 12 and make sure that you are able to maintain full control at all times. Continue training your Leo regularly, even after you believe the dog understands what is required. Repeating the training procedures helps you to maintain top-class control of your dog.

Keeping Good Control

•Do not be afraid of putting your Leo on a lead, even in the house, when situations are likely to be at their most difficult or when you feel you need added control. This may be especially important at the start of training (or retraining), when visitors are expected or at any other time when you need complete control or extra confidence. Always have something in your pocket to use as a reward for the Leo's good behaviour and to encourage good conduct.

•Do not threaten the dog into the control exercises. It should be firmly controlled, and yet taught in a friendly, non-aggressive manner.

•Do not avoid situations that the dog does not like, or where it has shown signs of dominance or aggression, although you must not put yourself in a situation where you risk being bitten. Alter the circumstances so that you can take control and feel confident in handling the situation. Start at a distance and work back to problem areas, slowly building up your own confidence and control.

•Do not be too predictable or over-repetitive in your daily routine or training programme. The intelligent Leo will soon start trying to take the lead role, anticipating your next move if you do so.

•Do teach your Leo to accept and enjoy being groomed. If it does not like it, distract it with a toy or titbit and very gently brush small areas each day, building up the volume of the area that you cover until you can touch the whole of your Leo's body. Grooming is a natural part of a dog's social behaviour and it must learn to accept being groomed by you.

•Do make sure that your Leo has plenty of activities which involve the control training sessions, games started by you, change of environment, excursions to new places, and so on. Join training classes, go to water trials, have a go at Flyball, Working Trials, Obedience or, if your Leo is physically developed and fit enough to jump, why not try Agility. You do not have to take any of these

Barking is a behaviour that can be controlled with a keyword.

activities to competition standard unless you want to, but the more you do with your dog the more it will accept your control and use up excess energy.

•Do stick to the rules if you want to maintain control of your dominant or potentially dominant dog.

Remember The potential to be dominant does not go away. You must control your dog and remain in control all of the time. A strong, fit dog takes any opportunity it can to increase its position in the hierarchy.

Keep your cool, keep control!

Hierarchy, Dominance and Other Dogs

If you want your Leo to live peacefully with other dogs in the family, it is better to start with a pup rather than trying to integrate a fully-grown adult dog into a family of other adult dogs.

To maintain overall authority, you must be the one that all the dogs see as being in control. If the adult dogs already know their places, let the new pup integrate and find its own level and allow the others to reprove it gently when they deem fit.

For your part, you must carefully oversee and make sure that things do not get out of hand. Do not make too much fuss of the new dog in the presence of the others, and always praise, feed and favour the top dog in your pack first to help maintain its position. If you can work out the exact position of each dog, you can help to keep the balance by awarding your favours and feeding in order of rank. If you start to reward the underlings first, then your top dog will feel challenged and be more likely to instigate fights. Your lower-ranking animals will feel elevated and more likely to challenge the top position. This leads to unnecessary friction and constant squabbling and, at worst, severe fighting.

A cage is useful when travelling with your Leo.

If you have two or more dogs who are aggressive towards each other, you need to work on widening the social barrier between them. This means following the rules above in rewarding and favouring in order of rank. However, you should over-emphasise this and look for opportunities to show rank order. This is not something that humans like doing, because instinctively we want to look after and award favours to the weaker animals. In short, we feel sorry for them. But this is not the way of the wild, and dogs react like their cousins, the wolves. If another animal is weaker in body or character then they will try to keep it there to make their own survival more secure. Even though this is not really an issue in a domestic environment, and all animals will be fed and looked after by you, some still see the need to develop strong hierarchy patterns.

If two males are a problem together, you can widen the social gap still further with the help of castration. If you decide to take this step then the more submissive dog should be castrated first. This lowers its rank further, and makes fights less likely. The neutered dog also stops giving off the scent of an entire male, and so the other dog does not see it as a threat. The learnt behaviour is still there, and castration is rarely a cure on its own for problem behaviour. Training must also be carried out with careful control of rank and favours by you.

Later you may wish to castrate the other male to help curb inter-male aggression with other dogs outside your home. But again, training must be used in conjunction with the surgery for it to be successful. Distraction training is the best means of training the dog, as described later in this section (see also Taking on an Older Leo, page 38).

Aggression in the Show Ring

If your Leo is aggressive at shows then you have to work hard to control this behaviour, both for your own benefit and that of other exhibitors. Naturally it is very frustrating and embarrassing if your dog continually lunges out at other dogs, but it is even worse for other exhibitors, particularly those who are out with young or vulnerable dogs. A good dog can be spoilt by the lack of thought and control of others.

If your Leo is aggressive, for whatever reason, you must first gain its trust in you. Much aggression is caused by fear, or an inability or lack of knowledge of how to deal with a given situation. Therefore it makes sense to build a foundation for your dog to cling to and respect. Training and character building will help you to communicate better, so turn to Chapter 12 and teach your Leo to work with you.

Together with this, turn to the sections which appear later in this chapter on distraction training and clicker training. These will help you to turn the behaviour around. What you should not do, at least to start with, is to put yourself and the dog in a situation that you cannot control. You must gain confidence, both your own and the dog's, before you go on.

You are not aiming to teach your dog to be best buddies with every dog it meets, which may never be possible, but to teach it to ignore other dogs and look to you for guidance. Once you have taught this, it is important that you never let your dog down. Walk away from other feisty dogs or owners who lack control. Teach your dog to watch you and do not allow eye to eye contact with other dogs. Watch other people's dogs; if they look at yours, make sure yours looks away and is distracted to avoid a fight or squabble starting.

I have watched experienced handlers, and even dog training instructors, allow their dogs to stare at other dogs and then, when a fight results, accuse the other dog of being the instigator, knowing full well that their own dog can be brought under control but the other handler will have more trouble. Often the breeding or bloodlines will be wrongly accused, when the dog simply is reacting by instinctive or learnt behaviour.

If your dog is not staring, a fight will not be instigated by your dog. If another handler moves their dog close to yours, calmly and positively move away, turn your dog away, move forward, do anything to avoid a confrontation. You can also ask the handler to give you more space.

Changing Your Leo's Behaviour

Distraction Training

It is not always possible to approach the object which is the cause of your Leo's anxiety. In these circumstances, we have to teach the dog to turn away and look to you for comfort or an alternative reaction.

Your Leo wants to please you, but you must be clear what you want.

Read Chapter 12 on basic training. The section on playing with your Leo can be of great benefit in cases of undesirable behaviour. Teach your Leo to play on your keyword 'play' and, in certain situations, you will be able to use this word to your advantage.

Find a special toy that the dog really likes, and teach it to turn towards you and the toy on command, because it is fun and enjoyable to do so. A good way to train this is to walk along with the dog on lead in an area of low distraction such as your garden or a quiet room in your house. Suddenly turn in the opposite direction and produce the toy. Be really enthusiastic and encourage your dog to follow you in the opposite direction. Have some tasty treats with you too, and give it one of these. When you have perfected this procedure in a safe area, go to a place where the dog might want to look at something, but not be placed in a situation where it would be frightened or difficult to handle, and test your training. Have it on lead and, as it looks away, say 'Play' and reel its lead in, giving playful little jerks on the lead to encourage it. Turn around and walk briskly in the opposite direction. If your training has been good, your dog will want to turn to you and the toy.

Continue this training regularly, not waiting for a difficult situation to occur. When out with the dog, always be fully aware of what is going on around you and be ready to react before the Leo does. If you keep alert, soon the dog will learn that, when it sees things it does not understand or that it might previously have barked at, it can turn to you for reassurance, guidance and fun.

Do not worry that in following the above procedure you might eliminate any desirable guarding behaviour the dog could have. Quite the opposite will happen, in fact. You are teaching the dog to be confident in you and your decisions. If you need your Leo to protect you because of a potentially difficult situation, simply change your attitude to one of alert apprehension, and your Leo's attitude will also change immediately.

It is important to be aware all the time. Even when the dog is trained you should keep going through the training procedure and reward good behaviour. This means you must be alert to recognise when the dog has been good. Once a behaviour has been learned it can never be completely forgotten; you can successfully use the above method to change your Leo's reactions, but you must always be alert to the fact that the dog could, given the correct set of circumstances, revert back to the previous behaviour.

Clicker (Sound) Training

Another excellent way of getting your Leo's immediate attention is by introducing a sound that means 'Food is coming'. As many Leos are 'treat food' oriented, this is a great technique to use.

If you don't have a clicker or something that makes a positive sound, you could use a single word such as 'Good' or 'Clever', but the beauty of the clicker is that it always sounds the same. It does not get annoyed, its voice never changes, and it is easy and instantaneous to use.

To teach the association, choose a time when the dog is attentive and interested in you. Make the sound, and give a food reward. It is important that the reward comes after the sound, because this is the psychology that we want to use in training. It won't be long before the Leo responds eagerly when it hears the sound, because it knows that food follows. Do this initial training in a quiet area so that you and the dog can concentrate on each other. When you are sure that the dog has the idea, vary the time lapse between sound and reward or the dog will learn that the reward comes after a set time and lose interest if it does not. Just like humans, an unexpected reward heightens the pleasure, and the occasional double ration would not go amiss! Also, just as with any other training, change your training place so that the dog does not think that this action applies only in a particular place.

Once your Leo has learned to respond to the clicker positively, use it to indicate good behaviour at any time and it will turn your Leo's attention to you when you need it. Don't forget to keep a supply of tasty titbits to heighten response when necessary. The clicker should not become a sound to get attention, nor take the place of commands and signals; it is an effective means of indicating your approval.

Unpredictable Behaviour

In my experience there is very seldom such a thing as truly unpredictable behaviour if you take the time to understand basic dog behaviour. Almost all behavioural patterns are predictable, even down to the fact that a dog's behaviour is naturally variable.

Leonbergers are often portrayed as easy-going, laid-back dogs, and most of them are – most of the time. What must not be forgotten is that they are dogs, and will act in a dog-like manner some of the time, and some situations trigger this more than others. Many owners become complacent and firmly believe that their Leonberger is 'bomb-proof'. As a dog trainer, I know that this can never be entirely true of any breed.

All dog owners should remain at least one, if not two or three, mental steps ahead of their dogs. Learn to observe and read your dog's body language. For instance when it stands tall and alert, it is weighing up a potentially uncomfortable or puzzling situation. Being a predatory animal it has two choices: fight or flight. Perhaps it might assess the situation, realise that it poses no threat and so transfer back to 'bomb-proof Leo'. But just for a moment, it was a real dog; if the situation had needed action what would it have done? If it is on lead, its option for flight is restricted. Therefore, if it feels threatened, it has only the other option – fight – and so a low grumble or even an attempt at attack is instigated and, in effect, backed up by you.

Many behaviours are the result of communication (good or bad communication) between you and your dog. Some of these are relatively harmless; for instance, go down on all fours and see what your Leo's reaction is. Most will read this as an invitation to play and join you with their back end in the air and front end bowed. Other behaviours can cause more of a problem. When you look lovingly into your Leo's eyes, it may take a while to realise that this direct eye contact should not be construed as a threat. Just because your Leo is used to you giving eye to eye contact does not mean that it won't take it as a challenge if a stranger does so. Some people seem to do this to the extreme, pushing your dog to the limits, and if you are not in control to guide your dog away and advise the person of their mistake, your dog may feel the need to take up the challenge.

Many people pat the dog on the head. This is a dominant gesture: watch two dogs establishing position and the dominant one will try to put a paw on the head, neck or back of the other. With training and constant handling, your Leo can forget that this is a 'dominance thing', especially when humans do it, but even the best trained and socialised dog may react instinctively occasionally.

The human smile can be interpreted by your dog as an approach with teeth barred – I need not tell you what could happen next! If you tell off a child, your spouse or partner, another dog or even another animal, your dog may read this as an opportunity to assert its own position while the underling is down and join in, and will expect you to be impressed that it is helping you.

If a dog is in pain and someone is nearby, it may think that what it sees in front of it is causing the pain and aggression may result.

These are only a few examples of so-called 'unpredictable' behaviour really being quite predictable and, in almost all cases, can be avoided or trained against as long as you understand dog behaviour and accept that your Leo is an animal.

If you cannot identify the root of certain problem behaviours, or if any

You may have to provide a place where a pup feels safe.

behaviours are difficult or dangerous for you to cope with, then do not hesitate to enlist the help of a professional behavioural consultant or qualified behavioural dog trainer. Sometimes your insurance company will help with payments if you are referred or advised by your vet.

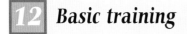

12 *Basic training*

Basic training is of utmost importance for all Leonberger owners. Some owners think that if they are going to train the dog for the show ring, then that is sufficient. Some are afraid to teach the dog to sit in case it does so when it is required to stand in the ring. This is silly; it shows lack of understanding and ability to control. All dogs, but especially large breeds, should be under the complete control of their owners and handlers at all times. The Leonberger has an active and enquiring mind and you need to stimulate and control this if you want a well-trained dog. Simply teaching it to stand and walk in show style is unlikely to be enough.

Like other dogs, Leonbergers do not come programmed to do as they are told by humans. Your Leo has no idea about the meanings of the sounds humans make, but it is receptive and continually learning. All that remains is that we are patient, understanding, pleasant, stay

As pups Leos seem easy to train, but lack of effort at this age means you will pay the price later.

in control of ourselves as well as the dog, and teach it the meaning of a few simple words in a way that it can understand.

Why Train your Leonberger?

One of the main reasons for paying particular attention to your Leo's training is the animal's sheer size and power when it is fully grown. If you do not gain full control from an early age, you will regret it later on. A Leo left to make up its own mind on how to behave will, sooner or later, make the wrong choice, and if this results in someone getting hurt this could mean the end of your Leonberger.

Most people consider it important to train the dog to do some things such as 'sit' and 'walk to heel', but to be more structured about training does not always come naturally. Many dog owners seem to think that the pup, whether it be Leo

Training is something that all of the family should join in and enjoy.

or any other breed, will learn the rules and fit in with very little input from themselves. You will be very lucky if this is the case. In most cases, the puppy's education needs considerable input from every member of the family.

Dogs need stimulation. They need to have their active minds and bodies trained towards a correct and acceptable goal. A bored Leo will be misconstrued as mischievous or downright naughty. Many young, developing dogs become fearful or feel uncomfortable in new or changing situations and, in the absence of proper guidance, react in the way which is most natural to their character or adapt other learned behaviour. This often leads to the dog showing aggression, growling or worse, because it does not understand how else to deal with the situation. Children, and developing adolescents especially, can confuse dogs because of their high-pitched voices and awkward or over-exaggerated movements. Lack of forethought, training and control on your part can lead to disaster. The dog's whole attitude to life and living with the family depends on the work that you and all of the family put into the training.

Training your dog should be a pleasure, not a chore. Make your mind up now to keep control, and to look ahead to all eventualities. Yes, you will make mistakes, but don't blame the dog for your errors. Simply count to ten, take a deep breath, and start again.

Voice and Body Signals

Using Your Voice
It is a popular misconception that a loud, masterful voice is necessary to train a dog, particularly a large dog like the Leonberger. This just is not true.

Dogs respond and learn best when addressed in a controlled, pleasant voice. They are excited and motivated by an enthusiastic tone and only learn to 'get away with things' if this is what the handler allows. It is not necessary to be loud. Even if you have a very quiet pitch the dog learns just as easily; its hearing is 16 times more acute than our own, so volume in normal circumstances is not needed. The only time that volume may be necessary is when you are working at a distance with the wind against you, or if the dog has its mind set on something else, but training to a whistle can get over this problem.

Occasionally you may find yourself in a potentially-dangerous situation when you demand an instant reaction from your dog. At this time a raised, more urgent tone will exact a quick response from your Leo but, if it is already accustomed to this tone, it is unlikely to detect your urgency.

A good way of calming dogs is to speak to them quietly using a low, soothing tone. Children tend to shriek and have naturally high voices; this excites dogs, so children should be taught how to talk quietly to their Leo.

Using Your Body

Leonbergers are very sensitive to body posture shown by both humans and other dogs. Often I have seen Leonbergers behave fearfully or even aggressively towards humans who have lowered their body posture and head position. The

In this picture Jean's body is upright – almost laid back. Draig responds by being alert and eager to learn. His ears are forward and his mouth is relaxed in a typical Leo smile.

Look at the difference when Jean leans forward. Draig is much more apprehensive, ears back, mouth closed. This is not a good emotional state in which learning can take place.

dog takes this as a threatening posture which immediately puts it into a defensive frame of mind. Therefore, you should avoid leaning over or bending your upper body towards the approaching dog when you are trying to get it to come towards you, as you know that this make it defensive and less likely to do what you want. However, quite often it is necessary with puppies to come down to dog level, so when you do this, kneel or bend at the knees, keeping your back straight, rather than bending over. It is better to lean back with arms outstretched and, as the dog approaches, bring them down close to your body. It is difficult to prevent everyone from bending forwards when they meet your dog so it is something that your Leo should be trained to accept over a period of time.

There are times when leaning over the pup is a good idea, as this helps to remind it of your dominance, but this can only be done if the dog is already with you.

Another way to use your body in training is to put yourself between the dog and something that it might be afraid of, excited about, or aggressive towards. Holding the dog on a short lead and stepping in front of its head, bringing it into a sit, and guiding its head up to look at you creates a physical block which then allows you time to break into its concentration.

Is the Leo a One Man/Woman Dog?

The answer to this question is, 'Only if you let it'. The whole family should participate in your Leo's training if it is to be a part of the family structure. The dog needs to understand that it does not follow rules only in the presence of one member, but that all the family, young or old, large or small, has the control and ability to train and handle it.

Your Leo should work with all the family.

In practice, often one person is the first to get to grips with techniques and training exercises which they teach everyone else. Leos are very adaptable, but this does not always go in our favour because they soon learn if one person is less consistent than another. In the long run, this is making a rod for your own back, as the dog learns to perform correctly for some and not for others. This then causes arguments within the family resulting in comments like: "Have you seen what your dog has done while you were out?" Funny how the Leo suddenly becomes someone else's property when it does not conform to the ideal!

People often think that the Leo is more likely to behave for the man of the house because he has a more authoritative voice. This is not so; dogs take more kindly to controlled and gentle voices, and this is borne out in the show ring where there are many excellent women handlers who have no problems handling the largest of dogs.

It is important that everyone in the household is aware of the rules, makes sure that the dog follows them, and enters actively into a constructive training programme. Even the children can control your Leo; just show them how.

Motivating the Leonberger

Motivating large dogs can be a difficult process, because many do not have long attention spans, at least not for the things that we deem important! But there are ways to the Leo's heart and, once you can find them, you will gain success.

We all work for some sort of gain, and the dog is no different. At the pinnacle of training, if delivered with enthusiasm, the dog is motivated by the actions themselves, but to begin with we need to find something that the dog enjoys to help motivate it into the actions that we require.

There are two basic motivators common to the whole of the animal kingdom (humans included), and these are food and sex. Sex is not an easy tool for humans to utilise in the training of dogs, and more often than not it causes problems. But food is a great seducer. We can also use play as a secondary source of motivation because this is how dogs learn to hunt for their main motivation – food.

The art of delivering the correct amount of inducement is a skill that you must work on. You must adjust to your own dog, giving little and often, and learn when to give and when to withhold temptingly in order to induce correct behaviour. If you give too much, the average Leonberger sees little point in trying; if you give too little, it soon loses interest. Titbits used as motivation should be kept and issued in very small portions. Tiny morsels keep the Leo wanting more for a considerable amount of time, and so extend your training time. If the titbit is too large, the dog has to take time to eat it, the novelty wears off, and you lose the momentum of the training exercise.

If you are using a toy to motivate your dog, choose something safe and durable, preferably that you can hold at the same time as your dog, such as a tug toy. Be careful of the Leo's strong jaws and make sure you keep your hand out of the way. If your Leo should come down on your hand, even by accident, let it know by withdrawing your play, turning your body away from it, and shouting 'Ow'. There is no need to hold a grudge or to chastise the dog further. Return to the game once you have composed yourself.

The Leo can be taught many things – even tricks for the film industry – as long as you find the right motivation. Jean Lane with Draig.

You should not allow the dog to run off with the toy as this defeats the object. You must be seen as the source of the fun, so keep the dog on lead and reel it in, or run backwards to encourage it to move towards you when it gets the toy. This ensures that you can enter back into the game. The toy should not stay in the dog's possession for very long, and if anyone lets go of the toy for any length of time it must be the dog and not you. Allow it possession for a few seconds only, and then playfully retrieve the toy in such a way that the dog wants to be with you and play with you. You may have to teach it to leave on command (see page 186), but do not give the command in a harsh manner.

Play with a puppy begins quite gently, but its strength soon builds as it gets physically and mentally stronger, so make sure you maintain control before the play has the chance to turn into a battle.

The Importance of Timing

Timing is very important if your Leo is to understand what you are trying to achieve. The dog's mind works differently to ours in that it thinks of what is happening to it in the present. This means that it reacts, responds, and connects things to what is happening now. Therefore, whatever your Leo has done, whether right or wrong, if you respond to this action after the event the dog has no idea to what you are referring. It will probably connect your words or signals to what it is doing (probably being good) at the time when you are reacting. Even seconds after, it cannot remember. Therefore, take action on whatever you are trying to achieve (or avoid) as it happens.

The Leo can learn that a sequence of events leads to a good (or bad) outcome but this takes time and positive teaching from you so that it gets the idea. The more positive and well-timed you are, the quicker the dog will learn. It is important that you are sure of what you are going to do before you do it, so that you can time things to synchronise with the exercise.

Read your dog. Learn when enough is is enough.

Using Keywords

The words we use for training I call keywords, because they are the keys to good behaviour. Humans need words, and the downfall of most humans from the training point of view is that they use too many words. This clutters the dog's mental picture and makes it more difficult for it to learn the exact meaning of one word amongst the many. But the Leo is clever and seems to manage to get the gist eventually, despite the humans!

Keeping your words and actions simple and clear speeds up your Leo's learning process, and enhances its ability to take in more of what you want it to. Once the Leonberger is attuned to learning and has learned to trust you, teaching becomes increasingly easy.

The Leo can learn to perform an exercise that it already knows on a variety of words, with only a few moments training to recondition each new keyword. This is because it takes its cue from body posture and attitude more than

'Sit'. Lynette Hodge's Khan and Purdy are learning early.

anything. The actual words do not matter at all to the dog. You could train your Leo to go into the sit on the keyword 'Onions' if you wanted to. The important thing is that you show or guide the Leo into the action, attach a word to this action, and reward the dog at the time it is performing.

Avoid confusing the dog by using extra words. Many handlers say 'Sit down', when they mean 'Sit'. This is fine until they come to teach the down position and say 'Down'. The same goes for 'Get down' to stop the dog jumping up. So now does this 'down' word mean 'lie on the floor', 'don't jump up' or 'sit'? I know Leos are meant to be bright, but even I would get confused!

So the message is – keep it simple with one word meaning a simple action or sequence of actions. Eventually you will be able to teach the dog to retrieve using one keyword, 'Hold'. This will mean: go out, pick up, come back, sit, give the

To start with, training should be in a quiet area, but once an exercise has been taught, change the environment and train again regularly. Vindor Stormer the Viking was Junior world winner in Barcelona 1992 and top dog of the Netherlands in 1994.

article, and wait. This is advanced training, but something to look forward to if you feel like taking it that far. But for now, let us start at the beginning.

The basic words and/or signals and procedures that the Leo needs to understand are: Sit, Down, Stand, Come, Toilet, Leave, Off, Heel, Play, Wait, Bed, That'll Do, Good boy/girl, to be groomed and touched and, of course, its name. Some of these words may seem obvious. 'Sit', for instance, is probably the first word most dogs learn. It might seem odd to teach your Leo to understand a word that means 'play'. But, if you play with the dog under your control and can turn it on and off when you choose, you gain far better control of the dog and experience far fewer problems as the dog's character develops.

There is more than one way of teaching any of the following exercises. Some methods are easier than others, and sometimes using a combination of techniques helps you to gain the best control.

Where to Train your Leo

When you first start training, choose an area where both you and the Leo can have some peace and space to concentrate. Only when you have mastered some of the art of control yourself should you try to train among the hubbub of the family and other animals. In the beginning, it is very difficult for the dog to concentrate with lots going on around it, but once you have gained its confidence and taught it that working with you is fun, you will find that the distractions don't matter so much.

Start training early, for all your sakes.

It is a good idea to attend a good puppy play group or dog training class if you are starting with an older dog. These are places where both of you learn, socialise and practise what you have been doing at home (see page 148).

When do you Start Training?

A popular misconception is that, because a larger breed matures slowly, training should not be undertaken until the dog is older. Some people leave it as long as 18 months before embarking on a constructive training programme. If you wait, you will soon observe problems creeping in.

Some sports and exercises cannot be trained too early because of the dog's physical development, but control can start straight away. Joan Mclennan with Flickan Fireball.

Basic training does not consist of an arduous schedule of exercises that might damage growing limbs. It is a programme of adjustment and control to guide a growing mind and body into the correct way of life.

Train your Leo from the moment you get it, irrespective of its age. It learns from you, the environment, and other animals and people around it, and you must guide it into the correct behaviour from the first.

More specific training can start within a very short time of getting your Leo. Give it a couple of days to settle in and then you should get started. Don't leave it much longer, because the pup is learning all the time; if you leave it to its own devices, you will very quickly find that it is making decisions that do not fit in with your idea of a 'good' Leo.

Train when the dog is alert and lively; not tired, or feeling uncomfortable from having just eaten, or needing the toilet. Observe your Leo closely, identify the times when it is naturally active, and choose these times for training and play. Early to mid-evening and early to mid-morning are usually active times for the dog.

A young dog's concentration span is not long, and at times a Leo's will seem shorter than most! Do not expect to keep training sessions going for very long periods of time. It is better to do many short sessions. You can still communicate, play, cuddle and guide your dog, and intersperse this with control exercise training. However, you should show no definite change in your personality or attitude when you switch from play to training. The two are closely related, and you and the dog should enjoy them equally. The rules of play are just as important as the rules of control exercises.

It is a good idea to use the run up to meal times for training, as the dog is generally more active and certainly enthusiastic at this time, and you can use the food to help with the motivation. The first exercise 'Sit', is often trained using a food dish carefully lifted above the dog's head. This use of its food and control leading up to meal times also helps to develop the correct ranking position for your Leo in your pack; it will understand that you are in control of it and its food and therefore be less likely to challenge.

If you want to prepare your Leonberger for a specific sport or for the show ring, some specialist training can begin early.

The Working Side – Left or Right?

During your training, you will be instructed to use a specific hand or arm to hold your lead or to guide the dog. This is because, should you want to go on to competition work such as Obedience or Working Trials, the dog will be expected to work on your left (unless you have a disability which restricts this). All the aids and instructions help to encourage your dog towards your left side as the working side. If you feel uncomfortable with this simply reverse the instructions given, and it works just as well. As far as the training goes, the important thing is that you are consistent, so once you have decided to use your left hand for something, try to stick to it. Don't keep changing or the dog will become confused and your training will be unsuccessful.

Once you have trained the dog to perform on one side it is possible to teach it to work as competently on the other side, but this is best saved for the more experienced dog and handler.

Traditionally, dogs are worked on the left as demonstrated by Fiona Parry and Bramble.

Leonberger Body Sensitivity

Different dogs have differing levels of body sensitivity. A playful pat to one might feel like a wallop to a more sensitive dog. Generally, Leonbergers are not extremely sensitive, but few enjoy being pulled around, and they tend to dig in their rather weighty heels if you try too much physical manipulation. Learn through your play sessions what turns your Leo on; learn when to touch and when it is best to withdraw or entice. Touch your dog and get in tune with your dog's body. I like to practise a little gentle massage all over my dog's body. This helps to build a confident bond between us, and also accustoms the dog to my hands being the bearer of good things.

Before you Start

The eyes, ears, mouth and body posture all convey what the Leo is trying to say.

The most important things to consider before you start are: make sure you understand what you are trying to achieve, think how you are going to approach your teaching, keep your attitude pleasant, patient and sincere, have your rewards ready and waiting, but out of reach of the dog. Do not blame your Leo if things don't go according to plan. The dog is the pupil, and pupils must not get into trouble for the errors the teacher makes!

I suggest that you start with the first exercise, even if you feel that your Leo can do this already, to get yourself and the dog into the right frame of mind, and to understand more fully the techniques and their concepts. However, if not already taught, it might be appropriate to bring toilet training to the top of the list. You may also feel it important to teach the 'Leave' command before embarking on other exercises so you have added control and ease of using titbits as rewards at the beginning.

If you experience difficulties with any exercise in particular, do not start the session with this one; try another with which you are more likely to achieve success. Work on getting yourself and your Leo into learning mode and being confident with each other before tackling problem areas. You do not have to get one exercise perfect before going on to another, but it is better to introduce only one new thing at each training session, and use the rest of the time to practise and perfect the things already taught.

Every Leo and every handler is different, so for some exercises I have given more than one technique to help you. In each case the first choice will be the easiest for most people, and normally my preferred way of teaching the dog. I always choose the easiest option – why make things complicated?

If using titbits for rewards, be careful not to create an imbalance in your Leo's diet. Take the titbits from the dog's normal diet, or at least allow for their nutritional value when preparing meals.

Ending an Exercise

At the end of each exercise it is important that your Leo knows when you have finished so that it can change position and relax. If it is not sure when you have finished, it will have to make up its own mind, and this will make it appear disobedient because sooner or later it will decide incorrectly.

A harmless Leo snooze?

Always tell your dog when to move by using a keyword 'That'll Do', or 'Finish', and at the same time physically encourage the dog to move from the position or out of the exercise.

If you are just about to end an exercise and the dog finishes or starts to finish before you tell it, put it back in position or take it back to re-do the exercise. It is important that it learns that you are in control and it finishes when you say and not when it thinks it should. It is very tempting for you to follow the dog's lead, especially if you are nearing the end of your session, or losing patience. You are cheating on yourself if you do this, because soon you will have lost the control that you have endeavoured to achieve. Therefore, always be sure that you have finished and make sure that the dog is aware of this too.

Teaching your Leo its Name

Teaching the puppy Leo its name might seem a simple task, but it is amazing how many puppies respond more readily to words such as 'Dinner', 'Walkies', 'Biscuit', 'Puppy', 'Oi', another pet's name, or even a family member's name. The way to teach your Leo to respond well to its name is to make many good connections with it.

The same applies if you wish to change your Leo's name for some reason. This may be the case if you take on an older dog – perhaps it has learned bad associations with its name, or maybe you just don't like it. Whatever the reason, it is easy to change the name.

The name is there purely as a lever to get the dog's attention and to tell it that we are talking to it and not some other person, animal or even ourselves. Therefore the association has to be a good one in order that the Leo responds to the next request or direction.

Each time you feed the Leo, call its name before giving any other instruction, so the feeding time routine could go something like this: 'Danny – Dinner'. The Leo is alerted by the smell and sight of the bowl. 'Danny – Sit'. The bowl is raised above the dog's head to encourage it into the sit position. If it has done this before, the Leo sits eagerly in anticipation of the food. 'Danny – Eat' or 'Danny – Take it'. The hungry Danny needs no further encouragement.

Adopt this same principle whenever the Leo is given food or a reward or whenever it can see that there is a reward to come. Thus it learns an eager response to its own name. Later, even in the absence of the food reward, the dog will turn responsively to see what is wanted.

If the dog is doing something it should not be doing, you can use its name to get its attention, but you should not get annoyed with it. Tell your dog what it should be doing, and when it stops the incorrect behaviour and is good, praise it. You must not continue to chastise it for its wrong behaviour because it will not understand and will associate your scolding with whatever it is doing now, which is paying attention to you.

If you often use its name in conjunction with a telling-off, especially if you speak harshly, the dog will go off the idea of responding to it. So be careful how you use this very useful word if it is to serve you well.

Appreciation Keywords

Once the dog starts to show some ability to do the exercise you can also introduce the appreciation keyword 'Good Girl', (Boy/Puppy/Dog). This should not be used so much that it obliterates the importance of the actual keyword that you are trying to teach. By this I mean that once you have an element of success, it is very easy to get carried away saying 'Good Puppy' instead of putting emphasis on the keyword. Then when you come to teach the next exercise and its effective word connection, as soon as you say 'Good Puppy', the dog becomes confused, because you have used this word so abundantly in the previously-taught exercise.

You will enjoy your companion Leonberger more if it is well-behaved.

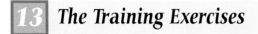
Exercise One: Play

Step 1 Find a toy suitable for your dog, preferably a good-sized rope or rubber tug that you can hold at the same time as the dog. Put the dog on a longish lead. If you are training a young pup, go down to its level, by sitting or kneeling on the floor. Hold on to the end of the lead or, better still, tie it to something solid so that both hands are free.

Step 2 Encourage the dog to play with the toy. Each time it takes the toy in its mouth, say 'Play' or, if you feel that the word needs more emphasis, try 'Get it', or 'Tug'. Choose a word you feel comfortable with, and use it each time the dog takes the article. Repeat the

Teach your Leo to play under your control.

word enthusiastically while the dog has the toy in its mouth. Anticipate when it is about to let go and stop using the 'play' word.

Step 3 After some practice, you will be able to identify the times when the dog is just about to take the toy. At this point introduce your 'play' word so that you are saying 'play' as the pup is on its way to play. Keep hold of one end of the toy and do not let your Leo run off. Keep it with you by reeling it in on the lead if necessary, or running backwards to encourage the dog to come towards you. Use a pleasant voice, action and attitude to convey to the dog your willingness and enthusiasm to work with it.

Step 4 Now you have the dog coming on to the article with enthusiasm, reinforce your control by stopping the game whilst it is still very keen. Take the toy out of its mouth, which probably you will have to physically open, or give your 'Leave' command. Move the toy out of the dog's reach and say calmly and firmly, 'That'll do'.

Step 5 Wave the toy in front of the dog again, and as soon as you see that it is keen, say 'play', and let it take the toy.

Repeat the above steps until you can say 'Play', and the dog starts to play, say 'That'll do', and it stops. It is to be expected that a pup will play more powerfully the more mentally and physically mature it becomes. You must maintain control of the toys; do not allow your Leo to get into the habit of running off with them.

The play should be done on lead or a long line until you are sure the dog will always return.

Exercise Two: Sit

This is the exercise that you are most likely to have started already.

Technique One

With this technique you do not have to manoeuvre the dog with your lead or hands. The titbit can be used to motivate the dog and lure it into the required position. I have found this the most successful and easiest technique with lasting control.

Step 1 Arm yourself with a good supply of very small, tasty titbits. Find a quiet place to train.

Step 2 Take control of your dog by putting it on a lead and collar. Play or give a titbit to get it switched on to you.

Step 3 Hold the food in your right hand, and the lead in your left. Show the dog the food and give it a piece.

Step 4 Push your right arm upwards and out with the titbit in your hand. Lift the titbit above the dog's head and slowly move it back so that its head tilts back, and eventually the dog automatically positions itself in the sit. As it comes into the position say 'Sit' and give it the reward straight away. Do not keep it in position waiting – this comes later. First the dog must gain an instant reward which it will associate with the action and keyword.

Step 5 After the dog has eaten the treat, encourage it to move from the sit if it has not already done so by gently pulling it forward, or clapping to get it to come towards you. As it moves say the keyword 'That'll Do'.

Follow Up Repeat the exercise as often as you can, but not too repetitively; don't bore the

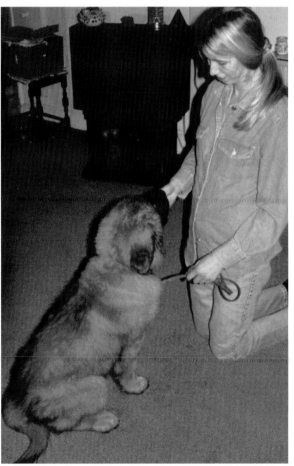

Stay in control but don't be afraid to come down to your dog's level.

dog by doing it over and over again. Two or three repetitions per session are ample. Once your Leo is getting the idea, change the position of your body in relation to the dog or choose a different place in which to do the exercise, so that it realises that you mean the same in other environments. Do not expect the dog to grasp what you want straight away. When you first change your training area, you may feel that the dog has not learned a thing, but it won't take long for it to understand if you follow the steps through and help it all the way.

After a while the dog will start to recognise your right arm movement, and take up the sit position without you saying a thing. Ultimately you will be able to use this arm movement as a signal for the dog to sit, even from a distance.

Once your pup has the idea you can come into a more upright position.

Technique Two
This technique requires more manipulation of the dog's body, so the handler must be very gentle and yet firm, controlled and sure of his/her actions. The Leo should not be frightened by the handling nor should it feel pressured. If you use this method, be sure that the dog is confident for you to handle it, and that you feel relaxed manoeuvring it. It is not always easy to manipulate an adult dog in this way unless it is very confident in you.

Step 1 Find a quiet place to train. You may find it easier to sandwich the dog between yourself and a wall to stop it swinging out and away from you.
Step 2 Take control of your dog by putting it on a lead and collar. Play with your dog, or give it some titbits to get it interested in you.
Step 3 Hold the lead in your right hand and manoeuvre the dog so that it is on your left or, if this is more comfortable, in front of you.
Step 4 Hold the lead close to the collar, making it easier to control the dog.

Step 5 Gently place your left hand on the dog's rump and raise your right hand with the lead slightly up above the dog's head to help angle its body into the sit position. As the dog comes into position say the keyword 'Sit'. Hold the dog there for a fraction of a second, and then say 'That'll do', as you move it off the spot by gently pulling it out of position.

Follow Up as above.

Technique Three
It is possible and often very successful to use a combination of techniques one and two.

Step 1 Find a quiet place to train and arm yourself with some titbits. Again using a wall might be useful.

Step 2 Put the dog on lead and collar to gain control. Have a game or give some titbits.

Step 3 Have the lead in your right hand and a titbit between your thumb and forefinger. Shorten the lead so that you are just 15cm (6in) or so away from the dog's collar.

Step 4 Place your left hand on the dog's rump and gently push it down towards the sit position. At the same time hold the titbit between the finger and thumb of your right hand so that the dog can see it. Raise your right hand, so that the dog's nose follows the titbit. As it reaches the sit position, simultaneously release the titbit into its mouth and say 'Sit'.

Step 5 Hold the dog in position if you can whilst it eats the titbit, gently releasing the pressure on its rump, but keeping your hand in position in case you need to re-affirm the position. When it has finished the treat, move it out of the position and say 'That'll do'.

Exercise Three: Down

Teaching the down has many benefits. It is an exercise which helps to affirm your dominance over the dog. It also teaches a high level of control, and is very useful when you want your Leo to settle down and keep out of the way for any reason.

Technique One
You may find it easier, at least to start with, to bring your Leo into the sit position before doing the down, using technique one of the sit.

Step 1 Approach this exercise by using steps one, two and three of the sit exercise.

Step 2 Bring the titbit down between the dog's front paws and hold it there until the dog flops down. It may take a while before your Leo tries this position; it may try to paw at your hand to get the food from the stand position, or put its front end down and keep its back end in the air. Be patient, and ignore all this until it comes down. As soon as it is down, release the food reward. Instant release will make the dog react more quickly next time.

Step 3 Repeat the above and, as the dog comes into the correct position, give the

Hold the titbit down until your pup flops into the correct position.

keyword 'Down'. Release the food, a little at a time, as it comes into position, so encouraging it to stay in the down position.

Step 4 Once the Leo has finished the treat, release it from the position by gently moving it or clapping to encourage it to move, and say 'That'll Do'.

Technique Two

This technique works best on calmer puppies and some older dogs. If you have a pup whose body is very sensitive and wriggles under your touch, technique one will work better for you.

Step 1 Play with the pup to get it motivated, but try not to get it over-excited. Place the pup in the sit position using any of the appropriate techniques.

Step 2 Once the dog is in the sit, push sideways on its shoulder. When you feel the dog pushing back at you, use the lead to pull in the opposite direction to the one you were pushing in, downwards towards the floor, and ease the pup into the down position. You can push the dog away or pull it towards you, whichever is the most appropriate at the time.

Step 3 Keep the dog in the down by gently stroking its back or tummy. Ignore any wriggling, keep calm, and keep your stroking soothingly gentle as opposed to quick and exciting.

Step 4 Keep the dog down for a few moments only, and then gently move it off the spot and say 'That'll Do'.

Using the Down

Extend this newly-learnt keyword and action 'Down', so that you can send the dog to its bed, kennel or crate. Put a treat in the area and encourage the dog over. Put the dog on lead, and place it in its area, saying, 'Bed'. The dog will find the chew and so connect its bed with a good experience. You can teach the dog to lie down anywhere in the house by taking it on lead and encouraging it to lie down. There are times when you want the dog to lie down, such as when you are watching TV, listening to music, reading or when visitors arrive. Spend time with your Leo on lead showing it what you want in these circumstances. It helps if the dog is relatively tired at these times because the weary Leo is more likely to be happy to conform.

Exercise Four: Stand

The stand has many benefits. It can be used to stop the dog coming forwards; to enable a vet to do a proper examination and take the pup's temperature; to keep still while you check it over and/or groom it; and, of course, it is a necessary exercise if you want to show your Leo for conformation, obedience, and so on.

Technique One

Suitable for all Leos. Especially good for wriggly or excitable animals.

Step 1 Arm yourself with titbits, get the dog on a lead and collar, and choose a quiet place to train.

Step 2 Show the dog the food, and then draw the food to the level of the dog's nose and forward,

Put your 'down' to good use and use opportunities to continue training.

until it comes into the stand position. As soon as it stands, say the keyword 'Stand', and hold your hand still to let the dog nibble at the food. With puppies it is easy to have your hand too high, and the pup will not come into the stand, so adjust your hand position to suit.

Step 3 Hold the pup in position until it has finished its reward and then finish the exercise by pulling or encouraging it out of position and saying 'That'll Do'.

Technique Two

Suitable for Leos who are happy and very confident to be handled. Not always easy to use on the heavier dogs.

Step 1 Hold the lead in your right hand close up to the Leo's collar, and put your left hand under its body, gently pushing back and up against its back legs to bring it into the stand. Encourage the dog forward into the stand by pulling forward with your lead. Hold the dog there, talking and reassuring all the time. Keep repeating the keyword 'Stand'.

Step 2 Keep the dog in position for a few moments, then release it saying 'That'll Do', and move it out of position.

Use a titbit to encourage your Leo into the stand.

Putting Things Together

If you have adopted Technique One in each of the above exercises, you can now put all three together, using a titbit to draw your Leo into position. Learn to manipulate your treats so that you can hold a few in your hand at a time, and keep pushing a fresh one between your finger and thumb. Link your Leo's two best positions together first, keeping it in position for moments only, and then drawing it into the second position before it gains its reward.

You will be amazed how quickly you can reach this stage. The Leo learns quickly with the motivation of food, and the positions are very easy for you to teach once you are used to the correct position of your hand.

It will not be as easy or quick to link the exercises using any of the other techniques, but you can incorporate the food rewards in all the exercises and this will speed up the Leo's understanding. Remember, the reward must come just as the dog is in the process of carrying out and, ultimately, going into the correct position, which is linked with the appropriate keyword and signals from you.

Use your left hand to ease the pup into the stand.

Incorporating Grooming to the Sit, Down, and Stand

Step 1 Collect plenty of titbits and grooming equipment and put them within your easy reach. If your Leo is on a table or platform, allow it time to sit or lie down to help it gain confidence before asking it to stand. Build its confidence by putting a supportive arm around it. When first put on a table most dogs become rather submissive or a little worried. This is a good time to show that you are in control, so allow the dog to look to you for confidence and reassurance.

Step 2 Choose whichever position the dog seems to be happiest in, either the down or the sit, and whilst it is in that position run your hands over it, let it see the brush and give it a reward.

Step 3 Repeat step two and then gently run the brush over the dog. Talk to it all the time and give a titbit whenever it looks worried. Remain in control and do not allow the dog to become agitated. Remember that excitability can be caused by stress, so do not get exasperated with your dog – keep your cool and keep control.

Step 4 Touch the dog's feet, examine its toes, look inside its mouth. Each time you do something, back your action with a titbit to show the dog that there is nothing to worry about. Repeat steps 1–4 until the dog is confident and relaxed.

Step 5 Once the dog is stable and confident, raise it into the stand position using your titbit in the right hand, and help it up by placing your left hand under its abdomen and towards its back legs.

Step 6 If the dog is new to the table, hold it there and reward, and then allow it to go down or to sit again.

Step 7 If you want to show your Leo, you can go on to teach it to stand for the show ring. It will not be shown on a table as some smaller breeds are, but if you are teaching a young pup, it won't do any harm to start there. In fact, probably it will have beneficial effects because you have the dog at eye level, and can control it better.

Soon your Leo will learn that this is a nice experience, even though it must remain in a controlled position. Do not let the sessions go on for too long

Grooming is not just about hygiene. It is a social activity as well.

to start with, as the young or inexperienced Leo will soon become frustrated, which will cause you problems.

Exercise Five: Leave

This exercise has many applications in the household. Once your Leo understands what 'Leave' means, you can show it things you would like it not to touch, introduce the word, and reward its good behaviour, instead of waiting for it to touch things and then telling it off. It is also necessary to teach the meaning of the word 'Leave', in order to take training further using the reward based-method.

Step 1   Arm yourself with a supply of tasty titbits. Take control of your dog on lead, and play with it.
Step 2   Bring it into the sit position and show it the food. Give it a piece.
Step 3   Offer a second piece, but this time stop the dog from getting the treat

This time the present was for Tyson, but if he does not understand 'Leave', then next time he might not be so lucky!

by holding it back with your lead positioned at the back of its head. With an adult dog, position the collar high behind its ears for better control. At the same time, say 'Leave'.

Step 4   After a moment, go forward with the titbit, give it to the dog and say, 'Take it'.

Step 5   Repeat from step two, but this time keep your Leo away from the titbit a second or two longer before you reward and say 'Take it'.

Step 6   Repeat from step two. The dog may be getting the idea by now. Observe its behaviour: if it pulls back from the titbit as you say 'leave', reward immediately. This is the behaviour you are looking for, the pup's ability to pull back and not to take unless told to.

Step 7   Increase the time that your Leo is kept waiting for the titbit. Keep a relaxed but close hold of the lead, in case you need to use it to stop the dog getting the titbit. Wave the titbit enticingly in front of the dog's nose; if it reaches forward, use your lead to restrain it and say 'Leave'.

Step 8   Build up the time that your Leo is expected to leave, bearing in mind that most Leos have a short attention span and, if you leave it too long without a reward, it will think it is not getting anything and lose interest. If it behaves particularly well by turning or moving away, reward it straight away. Vary the time that you prevent it from gaining the reward, so that you do not become too predictable.

Now you can incorporate your sit, down and stand exercises and use the 'leave' exercise to help you to build the time that the dog is held in position. Remember not to do anything for too long, especially if the Leo is very young. It is better to be successful than to enter into a battle with your dog.

Exercise Six: Off

Teaching the keyword 'Off' is similar in principle to the 'leave' exercise. Use 'Off' when you do not want the dog on furniture, or to prevent it from jumping up on yourself or others.

Step 1 Put the dog on lead, and take control. Have a game to gain its confidence and enthusiasm in you.

Step 2   Take it to a piece of furniture, preferably one that you do not wish it to get on to. Encourage the dog to get on to the furniture by patting it but, as soon as it approaches, firmly but carefully and gently turn it away and guide it back with its lead, at the same time saying 'Off'. As soon as it turns towards you, give a titbit or other reward. It is easier to control an adult dog if you adjust the collar so that it is high around its neck. You do not need to yank hard, but pull the dog sideways and it will turn away.

Step 3   Repeat the exercise to see if the dog tries to go on the furniture. Guide it away, saying 'Off', and reward as soon as it comes away.

Step 4   Approach other items that you do not want the dog to jump or climb on and control it in the same manner.

Step 5   Use this exercise to stop the dog jumping up at people. Take the dog on its lead up to a person and tell it to sit. Control your Leo with the lead and voice, and use your keyword 'Off' if it tries to jump up. Try to predict when it might jump and prevent it. Once it is settled, invite the person to stroke your dog. If it attempts to jump, ask the person to withdraw until you have gained control.

Step 6   Adopt the same technique if your dog jumps up at you, using the lead to hold it away from yourself, and incorporating the words 'Off' and 'Sit' to help the dog to understand what you require. Use a titbit to encourage the sit position. Reward the dog by stroking and giving a titbit as soon as it is settled in the sit position.

This exercise will be used many times during the dog's learning process and afterwards. Never assume that the dog understands that it is allowed to do some things and not others without being taught. Even if your Leo has not learnt to jump on people or furniture it is best to teach it the ground rules before it gets into bad habits. It should only go on to furniture if invited, and should never jump up at people.

Your pup cannot understand 'off' unless you teach it.

You may feel that it is acceptable for your Leo to jump up at you, but this should be taught separately and under your control. Then the dog will jump up only when invited. You will be glad you taught this control when you are dressed up to go out, or perhaps not feeling well. Don't forget that the cute Leo teddy bear pup is going to grow to be a Lion! It will get very muddy at times. It will moult, perhaps excessively. You may want to invite new friends or acquaintances who are not as 'doggy minded' as you to your house. An unruly Leo can lose you friends – a controlled Leo will undoubtedly gain them for you.

Using the 'Off' Word

There are other uses for the word once taught, such as stopping the dog following you on to the furniture.

Step 1   Sit on a settee, wait until the Leo tries to get on with you, tell it 'Off', and physically move it off the furniture. Then tell it to do something else, 'Sit' or 'Down' or throw a toy. Always have a reward ready for good behaviour, and remember that if the dog is not behaving incorrectly then it is being good. Don't be afraid to reward this, even if it is not acting under your instruction. You may find it easier to have the dog on lead to give you added control. Keep repeating until it gets the idea, but try to anticipate and stop it before it has even one paw in the wrong place.

Step 2   Once the dog has mastered staying off, you can teach it to come up on the furniture with you if you wish. Adopt the same procedure; sit on the settee, call the dog to you and tell it to sit. Show a titbit on the furniture and say 'Up'. Encourage the dog up, reward it, allow it a few seconds and then say 'Off', and guide it back to the floor, and reward it again. After a while it will get the idea.

Step 3   From now on, never allow the dog to come up without an invitation. When you see it approach, always say 'Off' and make it sit, even if you are prepared to let it up. Tell it 'Up' when you are ready. Do not cheat on yourself by allowing it up because you were 'about to tell him'. If this happens, make the dog get off, and get the exercise under your control.

Exercise Seven: Coming Back (Recall)

Teaching the word 'Come' is of great importance and is perhaps one of the most important keywords for any dog to understand. It is also one of the exercises most commonly taught incorrectly. For this exercise, a squeaky toy is a great motivator, because it is an audible signal to the dog that the fun is about to start, and you can utilise this later by taking the toy out on walks, and squeaking it when the Leo must come back. This toy should be kept especially for times when you want the dog to come back to you, so it becomes a special toy, much sought after by your Leo, because it is not readily available at other times. If your dog is more food-oriented, as many Leos are, a tin with titbits in that can be shaken so that it makes a sound works equally well.

Step 1   Take control of your Leo by putting it on lead and sit with it. Play with it, have a toy to encourage it to have fun with you. Also have some titbits ready.

Step 2   Allow the dog to go to the end of the lead in front of you, and then call its name and say the new keyword 'Come'. At the same time, give gentle little jerks on its lead, encouraging it to you. Repeat your new word 'Come', in a pleasant, controlled voice, and squeak your toy or rattle your canister. The Leo has no option but to come towards you if you keep jerking and reeling the lead in, but you should make the dog want to come rather than relying on the lead to do the work. Later, when your Leo is off lead, this attitude will be very important. The lead serves only to help guide the dog at this point.

Step 3   As soon as the dog is with you, reward it with a treat and/or toy. Coming to you must be a pleasant experience, and you must be careful that the fun does not stop when the dog reaches you. Repeat steps one, two and three at different sessions and in various environments until the dog is happy and confident to come. If it comes particularly quickly, give a double reward.

Step 4 Once the dog is coming happily, go back to your usual training place, which should be a safe, quiet, enclosed area with few distractions, and allow the dog to be off lead. Armed with a treat and/or toy as before, allow the dog to wander off. After a few moments, squeak the toy or rattle the canister and call the dog back, using its name and your keyword. Show the food and/or toy and encourage the dog all the time. Reward it with the food and/or toy as soon as it is with you. Remember the dog will be less keen to come back if you tower over it, so sit on a chair or kneel or crouch down if you are training a young pup. With an adult Leo remain upright, but do not bend forwards.

If your Leo ignores you, then you have tried to go to this stage too soon, your dog has learnt an incorrect association, or your reward is not sufficiently motivating. Start again at the beginning of the exercise, find a better motivation and avoid errors. The dog must enjoy your reward more than anything else around it.

Step 5 One of the biggest problems of getting the dog back is when it comes within arm's length, but you cannot reach it to put it back on lead. Keeping a good upright body posture will help to eliminate this, but so will the following extension to the 'Recall' exercise. Set up everything as in stages one and two, but this time when the dog comes to you, show it the titbit in your right hand and with your left hand reach forward and touch its collar. Then give the reward and release it with the keyword 'That'll Do'.

Step 6 Repeat the above, but this time introduce the 'Sit' as it comes to you and before it gets the reward. Use your titbit to bring it into the sit. Again the

Allow the dog to go to the end of the lead.

Reward the good behaviour with a treat or a toy.

Repeat the exercise off the lead.

Coming down to your pup's level will make you more welcoming.

fun should not stop when the dog gets to you, so have a game and then release it.

Step 7   Repeat as above but blend steps five and six together, so that when the dog comes to you, tell it 'Sit' using its titbit, and then touch its collar and give the treat.

Step 8   By now the dog is coming to you happily and sitting for its reward. The first time you try this outside your home, choose an area that is as safe as possible, away from other dogs and traffic. Although your training has been thorough, your Leo is still an animal, and things easily can go wrong. Instead of letting the dog off and expecting it to come back as before, sit down and go through your training. This new environment may be very exciting for your Leo, and it will not understand that your training applies here unless you show it.

Step 9   Stand up but do not start walking. Allow the dog to wander off, and as soon as this happens call it back and reward it. Release it again. If there is any hesitation on the dog's part walk in the opposite direction away from it, hide behind a tree, keep calling and encouraging, reward when it is with you and have a game. Then release the dog again.

Step 10   Walk a short distance, 3-6m (10-20ft), and call the dog. Reward and then allow it to go again.

Step 11   Walk a further 3m (10ft), call it back, reward, put it on lead and play. Walk a few more paces and release it.

Step 12   Walk a further 3m, sit down, call it back and play. Give extra rewards for fast recalls.

What you are now doing is building up pleasure in going out for a walk together. A walk with your Leo should not consist of the dog running ahead sniffing at trees and you simply following; it should be a team effort with both partners enjoying each other's company. If the dog learns that when the lead goes on it means the end of fun, or when it comes back to you the enjoyment has gone, it will always be reluctant to come back to you. If the dog learns that the fun starts only when it is loose, it will pull you to the park, race off into the distance and hesitate to come back.

If you have already created problems, or your dog is quite bold, inclined to be dominant or aggressive towards other dogs, start the training at the beginning and use a long line to control the dog. Allow the dog to drag the line behind it. This gives you the confidence of instant control, because you can catch hold easily. Once the dog is coming to you happily, start to shorten the line, cutting off 30cm (1ft) each time you go out. Eventually the dog has only a little length of line but has developed the habit of coming each time it is called. Do not be in a hurry to take off the last length but continue to use it for some time.

Never stop the training for instant recall because, if you allow the dog to start having freedom without being called at intervals, it will become more independent and less likely to come to you when you need it to. Therefore call the dog frequently and have fun with it. Even when out for a walk on a lead, call it to you and walk backwards, calling and encouraging it towards you. The more it gets used to doing this the easier your task will be.

If you do lose control, never scold the dog when you eventually get it back. This lesson will be learnt quickly, and your Leo will be even less likely to come back to you next time. Grit your teeth, smile (but do not reward) and resolve to train more thoroughly in future. It does not take long for us to get things wrong and teach a dog that there is more fun elsewhere, so relax and enjoy your dog, and remember you are a team – work together.

Exercise Eight: Walking to Heel

To have a Leonberger who walks on a loose lead by your side, without pulling your arms from their sockets or having you face down in the mud, is every owner's desire. The mistake that many dog owners make is that they wait until they are out and want to go somewhere before seriously considering teaching the dog to walk to heel. Start as you mean to go on and spend quality time teaching

Leos work well with motivation.

your dog what you want. It is very important that any owner of a large dog like a Leo has full control from the start, and it is essential that you concentrate on maintaining control all the time.

It is not good for your Leo to be allowed to pull into its collar at any time, unless under command to do so, because by allowing this you are teaching the dog that it is acceptable behaviour. I keep my Leonbergers on very short yet relaxed leads, especially when they are in training or in situations that might demand my control, such as crowded or exciting places. This means that I have instant control, and the dog does not have the chance to get the better of me because I have allowed it too much length of lead which gives it a greater leverage when it pulls.

You must also be careful if using training techniques that used to be recommended by most trainers, such as giving a good check on the collar or chain to get the dog into the correct place. This can cause serious damage to your dog's neck, as it does not take a very large check to knock the vertebrae out of alignment. This type of damage is not always easy to spot, but dogs may react by becoming agitated or grumpy when the pain is playing up. The unfortunate dog is then labelled as having a bad temperament or being unpredictable, when really it is in pain.

The best neckwear for a puppy is a soft, strong collar, and attached to this an equally soft, if not softer, strong lead. For the older dog, a half check collar gives added control as it closes with a central pull around its neck. I have experienced great success with all-in-one gundog-style leads which stay in place by pushing a stopper up the lead to hold it. If your dog is really out of control, then a halter style head collar gives peace of mind and ease of control until you can put your training into place.

To teach a dog to walk by your side takes patience, determination and, above all, a controlled and friendly manner. A young Leonberger puppy can learn from the start that the only way forward is by your side in a comfortable position for both of you. Training with incentives works best, and helps to maintain a bond of trust between you and the dog.

Technique One
Ideal for puppies and younger or very biddable dogs.

Set a mental barrier.

Use a treat or toy to encourage the dog into the right position.

Step 1 Choose a quiet place to train. Play with your dog on the lead.

Step 2 Guide the dog with its lead and a toy or titbit until it is by your side. Always keep to the same side, at least until the dog gets the idea. However, if you are thinking of doing any competition work in the future, then keep the dog on your left unless you have a disability which makes this difficult, as this is where they are always worked. Once the dog is in position, take a few steps forwards, holding your toy in a position so that it follows the incentive. Encourage it verbally using its name and pleasantries such as 'What have I got?' If the dog is too far forward, encourage it back by holding the toy/titbit back, if it is too far back use the toy/titbit to encourage it forward.

Step 3 Gradually build up the steps until you can walk across your room or garden with your Leo in the correct position, by your side on a loose lead, using the toy or titbit as a lure.

Step 4 Introduce a word that means 'walk by my side' to your Leo. Many people use the word 'heel' or 'close', but the choice is yours. Only say the word as the dog goes into the correct position, and repeat it while it is doing what you want. It is important that you do not introduce the word until your Leo is where you want it, otherwise it may learn an incorrect association with your chosen word. Do not do too much at a time, particularly when you first start training, as a Leo's concentration span is short. Getting 'walking to heel' correct will make the rest of your life with your Leonberger much more enjoyable.

Step 5 Once your dog is walking by your side happily, raise the toy or titbit out of its reach just a little and then give it back. If its attention wanders, attract it back by waving the toy or titbit in front of it. Watch its behaviour, and learn to give back the reward just before it loses interest.

Step 6 If you are patient and do not progress too fast, your Leo will get used to walking by your side and find any other position abnormal. Now change to another location so that your Leo learns to walk by your side in different circumstances.

Step 7 Gradually build up the distance the dog can do. If you start early, by the time the pup is allowed out following the inoculations, it will understand quite well. Even so, do not expect great distances from a young pup.

As your Leo grows up there will be times when it forgets what it is supposed to do, or something distracts it, but you must always be fully aware of what it is doing or is likely to do, and be there to guide it into good behaviour. Do not leave it to make choices that might not suit your plan!

Technique Two

This technique can be used in conjunction with the above, on its own when the dog is difficult to motivate, or when you have made mistakes with other methods. Sometimes, even when you think you are training properly, you can inadvertently teach the dog to pull instead of walk by your side on a loose lead. As your Leo becomes more aware of its surroundings it sees more pleasure in front of it than it can anticipate from the grumpy person attached to the lead. Ahead it can see fields, freedom, bitches, trees, hamburgers, fun! Look back up the lead and it sees nag, nag, nag, or nag, yank, nag, yank!

The way this training technique works is by taking away the opportunity to go forward, unless it is done in the correct position. You will train calmly and the dog can learn in a much more positive and favourable manner. If your dog wants to go forward it will very soon realise how it can be done, and your arms will not suffer too much in the process.

Step 1   If you have made mistakes in training, there are things that must change in you before you can expect your Leo to change. First, check that you are being positive, controlled in your manner and kind. Second, you must perfect

Talking to me?

your technique and know exactly what you are trying to achieve. Third, you must let the dog know there is a 'new you'. Take it into a room where you would not normally prepare to go out, place the dog on lead and collar, and adjust the collar so that it is high on your dog's neck to give you better leverage. Play with it to make sure it is happy with you, and offer a titbit.

Step 2   Get your dog into a sit position by your side. Look down at your dog and imagine there is a wall immediately in front of your Leo's head, and it must not walk into it. Now take a step forward. If your dog lunges into your 'wall', reach forward and guide its head sideways and back towards you with its lead. Now it should be walking back towards you, so take a few steps backwards until its whole body has turned and is coming your way. Walk forward again so that the dog passes you going in the opposite direction. Then, because you are holding the lead, the dog will turn to join you by your side. You need not say anything to the dog at this point except a few murmurs of encouragement. The main target at this point is for you to perfect this technique. You must prevent the dog from banging its head on your imaginary 'wall'.

Step 3   Once you have mastered the technique, introduce a keyword that your Leo can associate with the action of walking by your side on a loose lead. Choose a word that you have not used before because, if you have been unsuccessful in your training in the past, the dog has learnt the incorrect associations. A fresh start calls for a fresh word.

Step 4   Having chosen the word, put it together with the action by smiling down at the dog as it approaches the correct position and saying your new keyword. Do not say the word whilst you are bringing it back towards you, only say it when it is just coming into or holding the correct position. This is also a good time to introduce a favourite 'Leo treat' for your dog. Have a few in your pocket and hold them down at nose level so that the dog is able to stay in the correct position while it accepts your offering.

Step 5   The next step is to train in a different setting. The simplest way is to change rooms or go into the garden. Start from the beginning; don't assume that your Leo will pick up where you left off, as this is most unlikely. It needs to learn that you want the same obedience in this new location. So don't get angry, remember it is 'just a Leo' and will go into auto pilot unless you show it the correct way once again. In this new area, particularly if there is more space or attractions, the dog may be more of a handful, but all you need do in this case is over-exaggerate your previous routine. Instead of taking one or two steps back, move back with more conviction without, of course, yanking the dog's head off! Continue moving back until the dog is trotting towards you, and then walk forwards again as before. If the dog wants to go off to the side, you then take the opposite direction.

The rule is, whichever way the dog goes, if it is wrong, you back off, or at the very least walk off, in the opposite direction. Do not allow the dog to pull at any time, you must be ready to react the split second that its head is beyond your mental 'wall barrier'. If you feel that the distraction is too great but have succeeded in turning it away, have a game and continue to walk in the opposite direction to the distraction until you have perfected and are confident with your control. There is absolutely no point in inviting a battle you have little chance of winning, especially if you have a fully grown or powerful animal with which to contend.

Do not have double standards. If you decide the dog must be by your side then you must follow this through. Do not assume the dog will 'get it right', particularly if it has been 'getting it wrong' for a while.

Once you have perfected this, then you can teach your dog to pull, gait (run for the conformation ring), or even perform precision heel work. This technique will not spoil any of these, because you are being fair and controlled, and the dog is learning without pressure, which is the best way to learn. The technique will enhance your Leo's attitude to working with you and so will have a beneficial effect on its future training.

Exercise Nine: Toilet

Toilet training is easy if you accept the limitations of the dog and know that, given the opportunity, it will be clean if it possibly can. A pup's idea of being clean is not to foul in its bed or eating areas; adult dogs tend to be a little more selective. Restricting the young Leo's area of movement (let it sleep and rest in a crate or enclosed area) can help to get it clean and then it must have free access to the desired areas.

Some breeders give their Leo pups a good start by giving them a simple means of getting out of the bed area and into a suitable toilet area. Some breeders are very attentive and make a point of calling the pups outside to a toilet area when they wake and after feeding. But many do not have the facilities to allow such a perfect start, so your Leo pup may well be used to strolling just a short distance from the bed before defecating.

Whatever the case, you need to keep a close eye on your pup in order to teach it where you want it to go. Even an older dog may need training if its previous owners have not carried out their responsibilities.

The basic principle of training is to ensure that your Leo is in the right place at the right time.

Going directly to the toilet area

Ideally this is the method you should employ, because it trains your Leo from the start where it must go.

'Toilet' on command!

Best of friends? Shamoo and Alamo. Photograph by Pam Wells/Travelling Light

Step 1   Be aware of your dog's needs and try to anticipate the times that it needs to 'go'. Choose an area of your garden or yard suitable for it to use, away from children's play areas and similar places. Choose a word that will mean 'go to the toilet', for example, 'toilet' or 'clean'. Avoid any words that might be associated with other exercises or that you are likely to say in other circumstances. Some people say 'be quick', or 'hurry up', but these have obvious disadvantages, as you might use them when wanting the dog (or even the children) to speed up what they are doing. A well-trained dog will try to 'perform' whenever it hears its keyword, so be careful!

Step 2   At a time when your dog is most likely to want to defecate or urinate, call it to its special area and wait for it to 'go'. The dog will sniff, circle, and/or raise the base of its tail. As soon as it starts to show these signs, encourage it and, as it 'goes', introduce the keyword. Keep repeating this gently all the time it is emptying itself, and gently say how good it is. When it has finished, call it to you and give a reward. Clear up the mess and wait until next time. Each time you think it needs to 'go', call it to the area. Encouraging it in this way will help it to understand its environment and realise that there is a specific route and routine to follow to get to the toilet area.

Step 3   Be aware all the time. The young Leo pup may need to go more often than you had anticipated. This occurs especially when it first comes to its new home or when there is a change of diet. Each time the dog is allowed to go in the wrong place, irrespective of what you do after the event, it is learning that there is the right place to go.

Exercise Ten: Door Control

This exercise is simple if you set your mind to it and are consistent. Start by using the internal doors in the house, because there is not so much excitement for your dog and it gives you the opportunity to get to grips with the technique. It is a very important technique and should be mastered for two reasons. First, for safety's sake, as to have a Leo barge past you in the doorway can send you to the floor. Second, it is an exercise that helps in the control of dominance as it tells the dog that you are in control.

Step 1   Put your dog on lead, and set yourself up fairly close to a closed door, because eventually you need to go through it while still maintaining control of the dog's lead at the other side. Hold it back with the lead, relaxing and then tightening the lead slightly with an upwards movement, until you are fairly sure that the dog will stay back at a given point, and then tell it 'Wait'. As soon as you see it try to keep back, reward it and start again, as this is what you are trying to achieve. Do not push on further without reward at this stage.

No barging.

Step 2   Once the dog is stable and not trying to pull forward, repeat your key word 'Wait' as you reach forward to open the door a little. You should be holding the lead in an upwards position to control your Leo, and repeating your keyword. If your dog lunges forward towards the door, do not chastise it, simply close the door and start again. Be patient. Repeat step one first and, once the dog keeps its position, go back and reward it.

Step 3   Keep repeating steps one and two until you can get the door open sufficiently for you to go through. Once at this stage, take a step forward, controlling your dog using your lead and voice. Again, if your Leo goes forward, go back and make it wait in position. Keep repeating your keyword, 'Wait'.

Step 4 Soon you will be able to go through the door, but do not allow your Leo to move until you are in full control. Keep rewarding the good behaviour.

Step 5 Once the dog is stable, waiting at the other side of the door, go back and reward it for its good behaviour.

Step 6 Now the dog is waiting confidently at the other side of the door, call it through and reward it.

Step 7 Start again at step one. You may find that the dog is ready to surge forward straight away again. It is only by repeating the training procedure that it will get the idea.

Step 8 Once the dog is good at all the above, change doors and start again at step one.

Step 9 After each success, change doors until your Leo can wait at all entrances and exits.

Step 10 Start to practise the exercise without the lead on. Begin with internal doors so that your Leo understands that this is something that must be done both on and off lead.

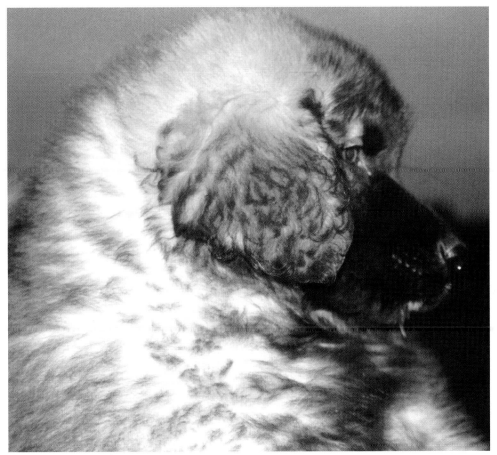

Manorguard's Fine Walk With Me (now Swedish and Finnish Champion).

Conclusion

If you were not convinced before you read this book, I hope that now you are well and truly satisfied that the Leonberger is a very individual dog, unlike any other. They are wonderful dogs to invite into your life and, once you have let one

'get under your skin', you will not be able to imagine life without a Leo.

Unfortunately, there are some drawbacks to owning such a dog, and I feel it my duty, before closing this book, to point them out. The problems start when you first venture into public. The time for every journey must be doubled, as you are stopped constantly by perfect strangers and asked, 'What a handsome dog, what breed is it? A what burger? Can I stroke your dog? How old is it? I bet that eats a lot.' And of course you feel honoured and compelled to answer patiently the questions as if that person was the first ever to ask.

The next problem is that your cuddly bundle of fluff grows rapidly, and very soon your saloon or hatchback car is far too small for your developing

'lion'. So it's off to the car show room complete with Leo to buy a car to fit the dog! But, no sooner do you have your new car, than you realise that life is just not complete unless you get yourself another Leo – and then there are two! But guess what, that new car which fitted your single Leo so well simply has to make way for a car big enough for two!

So as you sit, Leos at feet, checking your bank statement, admiring your large car outside, you realise that your house is far too small for your growing family, and pretty soon you find yourself contacting builders or, worse, visiting estate agents in order to provide larger accommodation for you and your growing band of Leos.

So be warned, Leos are infectious and, as bergers go – they are definitely more-ish!

Further reading

Bloomfield, Betty, *Care Of Newborn Puppies*, Hills
Johnson, Frank, *Dog Breeding: The Theory and Practice*, Crowood
Pryor, Karen, *Dog and Dolphin - An Introduction to Click and Treat Training*, Sunshine Books
Rahmer, Larry, *The History of Leonbergers*, Rahmer
White, Angela, *Everybody Can Train Their Own Dog*, TFH Publications
White, Angela, *Puppies*, TFH/KingdomBooks
White, Angela, *Happy Dogs Happy Winners*, Rainbow Publishing
Willis, Malcolm B. *Practical Genetics for Dog Breeders*, Whetherby

Leonberger Stud Books from all countries are available from your Breed Club.

EDV-Leonbergers all over the World - available on disc
E-mail joachim.steffen@coo.mts.dec.com

Index